Roast
Corn — OKra
~~Ford Hook~~ Limas / Peas
✓ Blueberry Delight — Banana
pear salad
✓ Spiced Cucumbers —
Tea
✓ Large pepsi
✓ plates + cups
✓ Forks
✓ Rolls
✓ Cake

~~Bag in Rubber~~

Finish Sunday
~~Blue Berry Salad~~
✓ pear salad
✓ Roast
✓ Corn
✓ Okra
✓ peas
✓ Apples + Dip
✓ make Tea

Stick Margarine

93
105
119
131
184
185

ADD A PINCH

CLARKSON POTTER/PUBLISHERS
NEW YORK

ADD A PINCH

EASIER, FASTER, FRESHER SOUTHERN CLASSICS

ROBYN STONE

FOREWORD BY REE DRUMMOND

Published in the United States by Clarkson Potter/
Publishers, an imprint of the Crown Publishing Group, a
division of Penguin Random House LLC, New York.
crownpublishing.com
clarksonpotter.com

CLARKSON POTTER is a trademark and POTTER with
colophon is a registered trademark of
Penguin Random House LLC.
ADD A PINCH is a registered trademark of
Add a Pinch, LLC.

Library of Congress Cataloging-in-Publication Data

Names: Stone, Robyn, 1972- author. | Dujardin, Helene,
photographer.
Title: Add a Pinch cookbook / Robyn Stone ;
photographs by Helene Dujardin.
Description: First edition. | New York : Clarkson Potter/
Publishers, [2017] |
   Includes index.
Identifiers: LCCN 2016044983| ISBN 9780553496413
(hardcover) | ISBN 9780553496420 (eISBN)
Subjects: LCSH: Cooking, American—Southern style. |
Cooking—Southern States. | LCGFT: Cookbooks.
Classification: LCC TX715.2.S68 S6746 2017 | DDC
641.5975--dc23 LC record available at
https://lccn.loc.gov/2016044983

ISBN 978-0-553-49641-3
eBook ISBN 978-0-553-49642-0

Printed in China
Book design by Stephanie Huntwork
Cover design by Stephanie Huntwork
Cover photography by Helene Dujardin

10 9 8 7 6 5 4 3 2 1

First Edition

TO BART AND SAM:
God blessed me beyond measure when
he made our little family. For that, and
for you, I am eternally grateful.

I love you more.

CONTENTS

FOREWORD

Robyn Stone just puts me at ease. There's no clearer way for me to describe what it's like to be in her presence. We got to know each other a few years ago at a get-together on my family's ranch in Oklahoma, and even though we'd met casually a few times before, our weekend on the ranch solidified a friendship that I have cherished in recent years. Robyn has a breezy, pleasant Southern manner about her, but she also a sharp, developed sense of humor that makes me laugh. Above it all, a strong faith and deep love of family guide everything she does. What a beautiful combination.

Like so many in our generation, Robyn grew up surrounded by the recipes of her mother, her grandmother, her aunts, and family friends. But she wasn't merely a casual enjoyer or observer of the food—she paid attention. She took mental notes, she participated in the cooking, and she honed those darn sharp cooking skills, even as a little girl. This lifelong love of food was ultimately what she channeled into her well-loved food blog, *Add a Pinch*, which has been a comfort-food, Southern-food, family-food, *good*-food mainstay for years. There's no way you can read Robyn's blog and not feel equal parts inspired and ravenous.

This cookbook is a delicious extension of Robyn's blog, and a perfect reflection of her love and appreciation for the significance of food in a person's life. It's also very clear that she cooks in the real world, for real people, in a real family. This isn't the kind of cookbook you'll reach for only on those rare occasions when you're having your boss over for dinner or you have to throw a cocktail party for a hundred of your closest friends. It's the kind of cookbook you'll use day in and day out, and at different times of the day, whether to get an idea for dinner that evening or just to sit and read.

Life is so busy right now. Everyone I know is scheduled from the time they wake up until they drop into bed at night. So, more than ever, I think we're all craving cookbooks that provide daily solutions for us. Robyn's cookbook does exactly that. You simply need to scan the introduction to understand what a hands-on, helpful handbook this will be for any home cook, whether novice or experienced. From clever ways to resurrect leftovers to freezer food tips, and from super-quick meals to slow cooker creations, the possibilities are abundant, irresistible, and extremely doable. Robyn's list of suggested pantry staples and kitchen equipment is also a great reference, making this book highly giftable for college grads or newlyweds getting ready to embark on a new era of home cooking.

At the heart of the book, though, are Robyn's recipes, which have stood the test of time for good reason. They are a monument to her years of cooking, her Southern upbringing, her love of caring for others, and her keen sense of flavor and style. I can't even begin to name the recipes in this book that are on my *"must make!"* to-do list, but here are a few: Buttermilk Mashed Potatoes (how brilliant is that?), Sausage and Cheddar Spoonbread (I think this is first on my list), Buttermilk Praline Cheesecake (never mind; *this* is first on my list), Brown Sugar Baked Salmon (oh, how divine), and—wait for it—Olive and Bacon Deviled Eggs. Talk about a feast for the senses. I love it when I read a cookbook and dog-ear so many pages that it becomes almost twice its original thickness! That's when I know it's a keeper.

Robyn Stone is a keeper, too. I absolutely adore her, and I'm so excited about this cookbook. I have a feeling the recipes, tips, and information contained within these pages will fill you with all sorts of comfort and joy. I know she wouldn't have it any other way!

Lots of Love,

REE DRUMMOND
Author of *The Pioneer Woman Cooks*

INTRODUCTION

I grew up on a small farm outside of Bowdon, a little town in Georgia that had a booming population of 1,700 at the time. Our farm was surrounded by the properties of my extended family—my Grandmother Verdie and Granddaddy Eual on one side, my Aunt Lulu Belle and Uncle James behind us, and another aunt, uncle, and great-grandparents just a bit farther up the road. It made for an idyllic childhood of playing outside from sunup to sundown, tromping through the pastures and fields, and running in and out of houses that felt as much mine as our own home.

Food was grown and prepared with love, and waste was not in our vocabulary. My family, like so many others, had struggled during the Depression, and the memories of those scarce years guided nearly every decision we made. There was a story that went with each tomato sliced, ear of corn shucked, or bean snapped. We had a deep respect for the land and for each seed saved and planted, as well as for our family, who passed along those stories to my sister and me.

Every springtime, my sister, Wendy, and I would help plant the gardens with our grandparents. Anyone who drove past us as we were planting would have had a sight to see! Granddaddy would lead the way, tilling the ground, followed by my sister, who would punch holes with a long wooden stick at just the right intervals for me to drop in seeds; then my grandmother would come behind us with a hoe, carefully covering each seed. The routine was repeated a few days later, that time with my parents leading the way. We helped tend the horses, goats, and any other animals that joined our small farm from time to time; we fixed fences and mucked stables; and we learned the invaluable lessons of hard work and responsibility.

Both of my parents worked outside the home—my mother went back to nursing school when I was three, and my daddy was a wholesale grocery salesman—which meant that Wendy and I stayed with our grandparents a good deal. The kitchen was a happy place full of activity, where grandmother always had something cooking on the stove or baking in the oven. We'd help her carefully pack bowl after bowl of food into a towel-lined basket to deliver to a neighbor's house or watch her glaze a cake for a birthday or reunion. In the summer, we'd help her prepare her Dill Pickles (page 218) to replenish the stores that had been depleted during the fall and winter.

After high school, I moved to a nearby town—our county seat, which in our part of Georgia we considered a big city (it had a whopping 13,000 residents!)—to attend college. While there, I met Bart, and we fell in love and got married. As newlyweds, we bought a small two-bedroom, one-bath house on one of the main streets on the edge of town. With more restaurants than I could've imagined in a short drive, our first year of marriage was filled with evenings on the town and take-out from our favorite spots.

When our son, Sam, was born a few years later, I knew I wanted him to have a childhood similar to my own. So we purchased a small farm outside of town and planted roots for our family. We brought my grandparents over to see it one Sunday afternoon, and as Bart headed down the old dirt drive, I heard my Grandmother Earlene gasp. I thought she'd been jarred too much on the bumpy road and asked Bart to stop. She reached over, patted my hand, and said, "No, honey, I'm fine. It's just that this was part of my grandparents' farm." Little did we know we'd be returning to roots planted generations before us.

As we settled into our new home, Bart and I both realized that we missed home-cooked meals and the care that went into sourcing ingredients and turning them into something special. We also missed lingering around the supper table and reconnecting at the end of the day, just as we'd both done in our own childhoods. Soon, I left my job in marketing to be home full time with our son, and I decided it was time to start recording the family recipes I most treasured as well as the new recipes I was trying out.

I loved poring over handwritten recipes I'd received from my grandmother, mother, aunts, mother-in-law, and friends. I felt even closer to these people as I cooked their favorite dishes and remembered how I'd been eating and helping cook these very foods since I was just a little girl. Recipes like Grandmother's Chicken and Dumplings (page 158) bring back a flood of memories. As a girl, I had to stand on a chair to reach the countertops, which Grandmother carefully lined with floured tea towels so that I could help roll the dough for dumplings. Or recipes like Mama's

Cream Cheese Pound Cake (page 210), another family classic that is very special to us. Even my son now knows how to make it.

I knew that I wanted to preserve those recipes and memories, that's when I began my blog, *Add a Pinch*, which serves as my personal electronic recipe box. Before I knew it, other people began visiting my website, leaving comments, and e-mailing me about the recipes, about the stories, and about their own lives. Now, more than seven years later, *Add a Pinch* continues to be a daily source of love and inspiration for me.

Add a Pinch has grown into a loyal community looking for delicious yet simple meals for their own families. And that community is just as diverse as a family—it includes newlyweds learning to cook, young mothers making their child's first birthday cake, working families looking for solutions to the "what's for supper?" dilemma, and grandmothers cooking for their extended families during the holidays. All of those readers from different walks of life love using simple recipes they know they can trust.

But the real reason I jumped so wholeheartedly into blogging is that I love cooking, and I love sharing what I make with those I love. Some things are just that simple. My own style of cooking puts a modern twist on the favorites I grew up with while returning to farm-fresh, homemade meals. I prefer to cook from scratch as much as possible, and have replaced many convenience foods that became popular during my childhood with my own whole-food, homemade versions. My food is flavorful, and my recipes are simple yet special. Those are the secret ingredients of making suppers that a whole family will love.

I like to write my recipes as if I'm sharing them with my sister or best friend, similar to how my grandmother and mother would have jotted them on a napkin or the back of an envelope to pass to a friend. This book brings together many cherished, scrawled-on-a-notecard, traditional Southern recipes but makes them simpler or more modern—versions of the classics that meet the varied lifestyles and needs of today's families. For instance, you'll find that I oven-fry instead of deep-fry foods as much as possible, decrease sugar when I can, and limit rich foods like heavy cream. These recipes embody my style of cooking in the South, celebrating the bounty of the garden, the freshness of farm fare, and the whole, unprocessed ingredients that the modern-day cook craves. I'm proud to make my recipes for my family and friends, and hope that you enjoy reading and cooking from this book as much as I've loved writing it.

HOW TO USE THIS BOOK

SMART SIDEBARS

Throughout the book I've included helpful sidebars that will help the modern home cook. As you page through, watch for the following types of suggestions and solutions:

Southern Hospitality: The art of hospitality isn't only for generations past! Just as my grandmother and mother cared for others by thoughtfully preparing meals for neighbors, friends, and family, I provide simple tips for sharing dishes with others and entertaining.

Leftover Makeover: We may not be in the Great Depression anymore, but the Great Recession taught many families to waste not, want not. By learning easy ways to remake a meal into a new, just-as-exciting dish, you'll be able to reduce waste and cost while still making meals your family will love.

Even Easier!: Sometimes you want to dress up a recipe for company, and other times you just want to get dinner on the table as quickly as possible. I share ways to make a recipe even easier, with tips on serving and shortcuts for prepping, so that any recipe can be simple enough to make on a weeknight.

Lightened Up: There are times when you may want to make a recipe a little lighter. I've included tips for carving calories with changes or simple swaps without diminishing the deliciousness of the dish whenever possible.

How To: These sidebars guide you through preparing many staple items in a pinch! I share tips for making homemade substitutions for such items as buttermilk, as well as fail-proof basic recipes.

HANDY ICONS

Throughout the book, icons will guide you to recipes that meet your specific needs and lifestyle. Look for these tags:

10 Ingredients or Fewer: Being able to make scrumptious and satisfying meals with minimal ingredients is always a plus for busy families. Though Southern food is often seen as too complicated or ingredient-heavy to whip up on a weeknight, the recipes with this icon all have no more than ten ingredients and come together fast.

30 Minutes or Less: Weeknights are known to be rushed and hectic, especially with all of the activities modern families are involved in these days. By providing recipes that can be on the table in thirty minutes or less, you can skip the drive-through line and enjoy quality time with your family around the supper table instead.

Freezer Friendly (FF): Want to know my secret for always having supper ready *and* being prepared to extend Southern hospitality to someone in need? Freezer meals! These recipes are perfect for making ahead and freezing , or for making large batches and freezing portions for later. I also offer tips on cooking and serving, so that you have everything you need for easy freezer meals.

Slow Cooker Favorites (SC): Over the last few years, the slow cooker has become a busy family's best friend. My recipes designed for the slow cooker, along with tips for converting recipes for slow cooking, will help you welcome your family with a delicious supper any night of the week.

FREEZER TIPS

These guidelines are in accordance with the USDA standards regarding food storage and safety when freezing foods, so you can feel confident in how to prepare meals for freezing as well as how to serve them.

Cool. Let cooked food cool thoroughly before packaging it. Never leave foods to cool on the counter, rather cool slightly, then cover and refrigerate until completely cooled to prevent food-borne illnesses.

Package. Portion the food into freezer-safe bags or containers, removing as much air as possible or protecting the surface of the food prior to freezing. These are the containers I use most often:

- SEALABLE ZIP-TOP FREEZER BAGS are available in a wide range of sizes, but I suggest stocking up on quart and gallon bags. Be sure to get the heavy freezer bags and not the lighter storage variety. Press as much air out of the bag as you can while you seal it.

- DISPOSABLE FREEZER PANS are great for storing one-dish meals and casseroles and are available in various sizes. I wrap the filled pans with freezer-safe plastic wrap, pressing it onto the food to prevent exposure to air. I then wrap well with foil and seal well. I love that these can go straight from the freezer to the oven—just remove the plastic wrap and re-cover with the foil before you bake.

- FREEZER CONTAINERS with lids are wonderful for storing foods like soups, stews, and chilis. Many are labeled "freezer-safe"; the most common materials are heavy plastic, glass, and stainless steel. Fill the container as full as possible, leaving about ½ inch of space between the contents and the lid. To prevent freezer burn, "burp" the lid to remove as much air as possible.

Label. Label packaged items with a freezer-safe permanent marker. I like to use a black Sharpie marker and write directly on bags or foil pans, and on freezer tape for other containers. Include the contents, the date prepared, and the reheating instructions. When labeling, consider how the item will be stored in your freezer. Sometimes you may want to label items on the top as well as on the side.

Store. Once your items are packaged and labeled, freeze them quickly. For items packaged in freezer bags, I lay them on a rimmed baking sheet in a single layer to quick-freeze them. Then for longer-term storage, I stand them on end (like books on a shelf). I also recommend storing like foods together. For instance, stack metal pans filled with casseroles in one area and flattened sealable bags of soups or chili in another. Such organization keeps your freezer neater while helping you quickly find just what you are looking for.

Serve. The best way to serve meals from the freezer is to let the dish thaw completely in the refrigerator the night before. If you're tight on time, run foods in sealable bags or freezer containers under cool water for a few seconds to loosen, and then reheat in a saucepan or ovenproof container. If in metal pans, they can go straight from the freezer to the oven. Just remove the plastic layer and re-cover with the foil; then remove the foil the last 10 to 15 minutes of cooking to allow the dish to brown. Use an instant-read thermometer to check that it reaches 160°F before serving. Frozen meals generally require one and a half times the cooking time to reheat straight from the freezer. Frozen cooked foods will keep for two to three months. Uncooked items will keep for seven months.

KITCHEN ESSENTIALS

A few essential items make cooking easier and more enjoyable. I've included a list of equipment that you'll want to have for many of the recipes in this cookbook. With these few basics, you'll be set!

EQUIPMENT

Skillets:

I hoard skillets! From those that have been in my family for generations to new purchases, my skillets and I are fast friends. If you want only one skillet, I recommend a well-seasoned 10-inch cast-iron pan; Lodge is a good brand to look for. You can find them any number of places, from large discount stores to the local hardware and online.

Slow cooker

These little electronics just make life easier! Many of the recipes in this book are written for a slow cooker, and others give that method as an alternative. You can buy the fanciest of slow cookers or the most basic, but I recommend one that has heat settings of warm, low, and high and a minimum capacity of 6 quarts.

Casserole dishes

In the South, we sure do love our casseroles! My grandmother had an entire cabinet dedicated to this type of pan, and she owned every shape and size imaginable. I recommend having a few of various sizes that are oven- and dishwasher safe. I primarily use 9 × 13-inch (3-quart) and 8 × 8-inch dishes. I also like to keep a supply of disposable casserole dishes, such as the metal pans mentioned on page 17 or inexpensive ones from thrift stores, for sharing meals with friends. Then no one has to worry about returning a dish!

Dutch oven

My Dutch oven stays on my stovetop practically all the time. A heavy-bottomed, wide pot with a well-fitting lid makes cooking chili, soups, stews, and roasts a breeze. It also works well for preparing ingredients for most one-pot meals and even for canning recipes, like Grandmother's Dill Pickles (page 218).

Knives

A good set of knives really does make a huge difference in preparing meals, but you don't need a huge collection. A chef's knife and a paring knife are the two most essential in my kitchen.

Baking sheets

My love for baking sheets is not quite as intense as my fondness for skillets, but it's close! They are a workhorse in the kitchen. I use 18 × 13-inch rimmed baking sheets (also called half sheet pans) for baking everything from one-pan meals (page 96) to a pan of biscuits.

Measuring cups and spoons

It is important to be able to properly measure ingredients. You'll need at least one set each of liquid and dry measuring cups and a good, sturdy set of measuring spoons.

Mason jars

Mason jars are just indispensable in my kitchen, whether I'm preserving Pepper Jelly (page 220), storing homemade Chicken Stock (page 104) or Homemade Fresh Tomato Sauce (page 229), or shaking up a salad dressing, I recommend having a supply of various sizes, from half pint to quart.

Wooden spoons

My grandmother taught me never to use metal utensils in my pots and pans while cooking, since they can scar my pans. Wooden spoons are perfect for mixing, stirring, cooking, and serving. They can last a lifetime (or lifetimes!) when taken care of properly, which means hand washing and drying.

Mixer

I have both a stand mixer and a handheld mixer, but one or the other will do. Having a stand mixer makes some tasks much easier, like making dough for Bart's Cinnamon Rolls (page 186) and Boots Butler's Yeast Rolls (page 182). A hand-held mixer makes quick work of tasks for other recipes, like the Mile-High Meringue in Lulu Belle's Lemon Meringue Pie (page 190).

Box grater

My box grater is one of my most used utensils. I use it to grate cheeses right off the block for recipes like Southern Pimento Cheese (page 34), grate citrus zest, and more.

Spice grinder

Once I discovered how much better freshly ground black pepper tastes than the preground store-bought stuff, I was smitten. I use my spice grinder routinely for making my Stone House Seasoning (page 226), which you'll find in many recipes.

PANTRY

Kosher salt

I love using coarse kosher salt in my cooking. It has a clean taste, and I think that its larger flakes make it harder to oversalt dishes. Kosher salt can take a dish from okay to great. If you use regular table salt, start with half the amount called for in the recipe and adjust to your preference.

Butter

You'll notice that I call for salted butter in my recipes. Here's why: Salt is a preservative, allowing salted butter to last up to three months in the refrigerator, while unsalted butter lasts only about a month. If you prefer to use unsalted butter, adjust the amount of salt called for in the recipe to your preference. I use Land O'Lakes butter with great success.

Flour

Any all-purpose flour will do just fine in my recipes, though I like White Lily the best. Lower in protein than most flours, White Lily makes for flakier biscuits and piecrusts and moist, tender cakes.

Oil mister

I use oil misters filled with my favorite olive oil to lightly coat pans to prevent sticking. If you do not have an oil mister, you can use your favorite cooking spray instead.

Baking spray

When baking, I recommend preparing the baking pan with a baking spray that contains flour. I like Baker's Joy brand. You can also grease with butter and lightly dust with flour.

Seasonings

You'll notice that I often use a house seasoning (page 226) in my cooking. I like to make a big batch of it so I always have some handy beside my stovetop. I can't recommend it enough! Experiment with seasonings to find your own favorite blend, and you can elevate the flavor of a wide variety of dishes in a snap.

Homemade sauces, soups, and such

I like to make Homemade Fresh Tomato Sauce (page 229), Cream of Chicken Soup (page 108), Chicken Stock (page 104), and similar staples from scratch. I generally make these in large batches and freeze them for later use. That way, I know exactly what I'm eating in all of my dishes. If you substitute store-bought versions, choose ones with minimal ingredients that are the best match for those listed in the recipes.

STARTERS
& SNACKS

SOUTHERN CHEESE CRACKERS THREE WAYS

MAKES 48 TO 60 CRACKERS

1 (8-ounce) block of sharp Cheddar cheese, shredded (about 2 cups)

8 tablespoons (1 stick) salted butter, softened

1 teaspoon kosher salt

½ teaspoon cayenne pepper

¼ teaspoon freshly ground black pepper

⅛ teaspoon garlic powder

1½ cups all-purpose flour

freezer friendly
You can store unbaked cracker dough in the freezer for up to 2 months to be ahead of the game. Wrap it well in plastic wrap, then drop it into a sealable freezer bag. Simply thaw in the refrigerator overnight, slice, and bake as directed. You can also refrigerate the dough for up to a week before baking.

These crackers make a perfect nibble to serve when company comes. I love the classic version, but the pecan and pimento cheese variations are an easy switch for serving with fruit, as part of a cheese board, or with Black-Eyed Pea Hummus (page 38). They are also a great addition to soups and salads. Here's the deal though: You can never eat just one—at least, I've never met anyone who could!

1   Using an electric hand mixer, beat together the cheese and butter until fluffy, about 3 minutes. Mix in the salt, cayenne, black pepper, and garlic powder. Add the flour ½ cup at a time, stirring after each addition, until the ingredients are well combined and a dough forms. Turn the dough out onto a piece of parchment paper or plastic wrap and shape it into a 1-inch-diameter log. Twist the ends of the parchment paper to seal. Refrigerate for 30 minutes.

2   Preheat the oven to 375°F. Line a baking sheet with parchment paper or a silicone baking mat.

3   Remove the dough from the refrigerator, unwrap, and place on a cutting board. Cut the log into ⅛-inch-thick slices and place ¼ inch apart on the prepared baking sheet.

4   Bake until light golden brown, about 15 minutes. Transfer to a wire rack and let cool completely. The crackers will keep in an airtight container for up to 1 week.

NOTE I prefer to grate my own cheese right off the block. If you use preshredded cheese, you may have stiffer dough. If so, gradually add 1 to 2 tablespoons ice water until it reaches the right consistency.

PECAN CHEESE CRACKERS
Add ½ cup finely chopped pecans.

PIMENTO CHEESE CRACKERS
Add 1 cup Southern Pimento Cheese (page 34) and decrease the amount of grated sharp Cheddar cheese to 1 cup. Decrease the cayenne to ¼ teaspoon.

southern hospitality

There's nothing like giving homemade treats as hostess gifts. I also love to make all three varieties of these delicious nibbles to give to friends and family during the holidays. They are always welcome!

CRANBERRY CHICKEN BITES

MAKES 4 DOZEN

1 tablespoon olive oil

2 (4-ounce) skinless, boneless chicken breasts

1 (8-ounce) package cream cheese, at room temperature

8 ounces goat cheese, at room temperature

1 cup finely chopped reduced sugar dried cranberries

¼ cup finely chopped scallions

¼ teaspoon garlic powder

½ teaspoon kosher salt

2 cups finely chopped nuts (pecans, walnuts, almonds, or pistachios)

Crackers and fruit, for serving

Based on Mama's chicken cheese ball that she made for so many holidays, parties, and showers, these are two-bite treats that are as gorgeous to look at as they are scrumptious to eat. Her original recipe used canned chicken, two blocks of cream cheese, and mayonnaise, all formed into a large ball. While it was absolutely delicious, it was also indulgent. I've updated the recipe to use home-cooked chicken and lighter, tangier goat cheese in place of some of the cream cheese, and I've portioned the mixture into individual truffle-sized bites. That way, everyone gets their own!

1   Preheat the oven to 400°F. Coat a rimmed baking sheet with the olive oil.

2   Arrange the chicken breasts on the baking sheet and cover loosely with a piece of parchment paper or foil. Bake until a thermometer inserted in the thickest part of the chicken registers 165°F and the juices run clear when the flesh is pricked with a sharp knife, about 30 minutes. Let the chicken cool and then chop finely.

3   In a medium bowl, combine the chicken, cream cheese, goat cheese, cranberries, scallions, garlic powder, salt, and 1 cup of the nuts. Scoop out tablespoons of the mixture and roll into balls, then roll the balls in the remaining nuts. Refrigerate in an airtight container or tightly wrapped for 1 hour or up to 3 days before serving.

4   When ready to serve, let stand at room temperature for 15 minutes. Serve with crackers and fruit.

freezer friendly

Place the prepared chicken bites on a parchment paper–lined baking sheet and freeze for 30 minutes. Transfer to a sealable freezer bag, remove as much air as possible, and freeze for up to 2 months. The day you want to serve them, arrange the bites on a serving tray, cover with plastic wrap, and thaw in the refrigerator, at least 4 hours, until time to serve.

even easier!

This recipe can also be transformed into a great chicken salad to serve in lettuce cups. Mix in all of the nuts, skip the step of rolling the chicken mixture into balls, and instead spoon it into Bibb lettuce leaves.

OLIVE *and* BACON DEVILED EGGS

12 large eggs, hard-boiled (see sidebar)

5 tablespoons mayonnaise

1 teaspoon Dijon mustard

¼ teaspoon kosher salt

¼ teaspoon freshly ground black pepper

10 pimento-stuffed green olives, sliced

3 slices of cooked bacon, crumbled or roughly chopped

Deviled eggs have to be one of the most versatile dishes in the world. So easy to prepare, they always make an appearance at my house during the holidays and at showers, reunions, and parties. While we love deviled eggs just about any way that you can think to make them, this olive and bacon version is one of my favorites.

1 Slice the hard-boiled eggs in half lengthwise and pop the yolks into a medium bowl. Using a fork, mash the yolks. Stir in the mayonnaise, mustard, salt, and pepper.

2 Using a spoon or a pastry bag fitted with a large star tip, fill each egg white with the egg yolk mixture. Arrange the eggs on a platter and top each with a slice of olive and bacon. Cover and refrigerate for at least 30 minutes before serving.

HOW TO *hard-boil eggs*

To boil eggs that peel easily every time, I still use the method I learned in my high school home economics class. Arrange the eggs (however many you're cooking, but be sure not to overcrowd the pan) in a single layer in a heavy-bottomed saucepan and add cool, fresh water to cover by 1 to 2 inches. Add ¼ teaspoon baking soda and bring to a boil over medium-low heat. Boil for 1 minute, then cover and remove the pan from the heat. Let sit for 12 minutes. Using a slotted spoon, transfer the eggs to a bowl of ice water to stop the cooking. They peel perfectly for me every single time!

OVEN-FRIED GREEN TOMATO CAPRESE STACKS

SERVES 4 TO 6

Oil mister or cooking spray

4 large green tomatoes, cut into ½-inch-thick slices

½ cup buttermilk

2 large eggs

1 cup cornmeal

1 cup all-purpose flour

1 teaspoon kosher salt

½ teaspoon freshly ground black pepper

6 tablespoons olive oil

8 ounces mozzarella cheese, cut into ½-inch-thick slices

12 whole basil leaves

Balsamic Reduction (recipe follows)

In early summer, before the tomatoes show even a speck of pink, you'll find me in the garden picking them. I swear I can still hear my daddy lecturing me for picking so many before they had a chance to ripen. He'd stop by our little house, as he did most afternoons, and, with a hint of laughter in his voice, say, "You'll never even have enough tomatoes for a sandwich if you keep picking them the minute the plant starts blooming." But heavens, they sure do shine in this dish. Lighter and so much easier than traditional deep-fried green tomatoes, these still offer that familiar crunch when you take a bite. They're perfect as an appetizer when you have company, but I also love them as a weeknight side dish with supper.

1   Preheat the oven to 450°F. Line a baking sheet with foil (to catch drippings) and place a wire rack on the baking sheet. Lightly spray the rack with oil. Line a second baking sheet with paper towels.

2   Place the tomato slices on the baking sheet lined with paper towels. Cover the tomatoes with additional paper towels and pat dry.

3   In a shallow dish, whisk together the buttermilk and eggs. In a separate shallow dish, whisk together the cornmeal, flour, salt, and pepper. Working in batches, dip the tomato slices into the buttermilk mixture and then into the cornmeal mixture, making sure that both sides and the edges are well coated.

4   In a medium skillet set over medium heat, heat 3 tablespoons of the oil until it begins to shimmer, about 1 minute. Cook the tomatoes until lightly browned on one side, about 1 minute. Flip to brown the other side, 1 more minute. Transfer to the prepared wire rack. Repeat with the remaining tomatoes. Bake until fork-tender, about 20 minutes.

(recipe continues)

5 Assemble stacks by placing one tomato slice on a plate. Top with a slice of mozzarella and then a basil leaf. Repeat with another tomato slice, piece of mozzarella, and basil leaf, and top with a final tomato slice. Repeat with the remaining ingredients. Drizzle with balsamic reduction and serve.

BALSAMIC REDUCTION

MAKES ½ CUP

1 cup balsamic vinegar

In a small nonreactive saucepan set over low heat, bring the vinegar to a simmer. Let simmer until the vinegar reduces by more than half and coats the back of a spoon, about 15 minutes. Remove the pan from the heat and let cool. The reduction will keep in an airtight container in the refrigerator for up to 3 weeks.

even easier!

If you want to skip the stacking, you can easily turn these ingredients into a lush and satisfying salad. Arrange 2 cups mixed salad greens in a bowl, then add ½ cup halved cherry tomatoes, the fried green tomatoes, mozzarella slices, and torn basil. Top with balsamic vinegar (instead of the reduction) and olive oil.

SPICY ROSEMARY ROASTED NUTS

MAKES ABOUT 4 CUPS

1 pound (about 4 cups) pecan halves

4 tablespoons (½ stick) salted butter

2 tablespoons chopped fresh rosemary

1 teaspoon kosher salt

½ teaspoon cayenne pepper

The combination of fresh herbs and spices in these roasted nuts makes for a delicious nibble that's perfect when entertaining, watching a game, or simply having an afternoon treat. I also love making batches to share with friends and neighbors or to take as hostess gifts.

1   Preheat the oven to 300°F.

2   Spread the pecans in a single layer on a rimmed baking sheet. Break the butter into small pieces and scatter them over the nuts. Sprinkle the rosemary, salt, and cayenne over the pecans.

3   Bake until browned and fragrant, about 20 minutes, stirring halfway through. Remove the pan from the oven and let cool for about 5 minutes before serving.

leftover makeover

I'm not certain you'll ever have leftovers of these spicy pecans, but I can't urge you enough to toss them into my Tarragon Chicken Salad (page 82). Talk about scrumptious!

variation

SWEET AND SPICY MIXED NUTS

Spread 1 cup each raw pecan halves, walnut halves, almonds, and cashews in a single layer on a rimmed baking sheet. Omit the butter. Replace the rosemary with 2 tablespoons honey, and combine it with the salt and cayenne before pouring the mixture over the nuts. Bake as directed.

SOUTHERN PIMENTO CHEESE

SERVES 6 TO 8

1 (8-ounce) block of sharp Cheddar cheese, grated (about 2 cups)

1 (8-ounce) block of mild Cheddar cheese, grated (about 2 cups)

¼ cup cream cheese, at room temperature

2 tablespoons Greek yogurt

1 (4-ounce) jar diced pimentos, drained, 2 tablespoons liquid reserved

¼ teaspoon Stone House Seasoning (page 226)

2 to 3 tablespoons mayonnaise (optional)

My grandmother made her pimento cheese the old-fashioned way—she had a meat grinder dedicated to the task of grinding her cheese. As a little girl, I was fascinated watching the process, and it made the most delicious pimento cheese I've ever tasted to this day. While I don't grind my cheeses with a meat grinder, I do like to buy blocks of Cheddar to grate myself; it makes a big difference in the texture. I also lightened up the recipe a bit by decreasing the cream cheese and adding a bit of Greek yogurt. If you want to make it Grandmother Verdie's way, just use a whole package (8 ounces) of cream cheese and leave out the yogurt and pimento juice.

1   In a medium bowl, using a hand mixer, beat together the Cheddar cheeses, cream cheese, yogurt, and liquid from the pimentos until creamy and fluffy, about 3 minutes. Stir in the pimentos and seasoning mix. If you prefer your pimento cheese to be a bit thinner for spreading, add the mayonnaise.

2   The cheese will keep in an airtight container in the refrigerator for 1 week.

southern hospitality

If there is any more iconic Southern spread, I can't think of it. Pimento cheese is lovely served in a pretty bowl, surrounded with crackers and celery. It is also delicious spread on a slice of bread for an open-faced BLT sandwich. I think you'll love it!

ROASTED FIGS *with* GOAT CHEESE AND NUTS

SERVES 6 TO 8

12 figs, halved

¼ cup crumbled goat cheese

¼ cup chopped pecans

Honey, to taste

I've always adored figs. As a young girl, I'd volunteer to pick them for Mama and Grandmother to make their fig preserves—one would go into the basket for the preserves and the next, into my mouth. I still can't get enough of figs when they are in season, and this quick little appetizer is one of my favorite ways to serve them. If the figs are ripe enough, you won't need much honey. You can also use ripe peaches or plums.

1   Preheat the oven to 325°F. Line a baking sheet with parchment paper.

2   Place the figs on the lined baking sheet, cut sides up, and bake until soft and heated through, about 10 minutes. Remove the pan from the oven and top with the goat cheese and pecans. Drizzle with honey. Bake until the toppings are warm, about 3 more minutes. Serve warm.

leftover makeover

ROASTED FIG TOAST

If—and this is a mighty big if—you happen to have any of these roasted figs left over, smear them onto a toasted biscuit or baguette. Oh my goodness gracious, talk about heavenly!

BLACK-EYED PEA HUMMUS

MAKES 1½ CUPS

¼ cup fresh lemon juice

¼ cup tahini

3 tablespoons olive oil

1¼ cups black-eyed peas, well-cooked and drained (see sidebar)

1 small garlic clove, minced

½ teaspoon ground cumin

½ teaspoon kosher salt

A Southern update to classic hummus, this is one dip that I can't get enough of! I love to serve it with cucumber slices, celery, pepper slices, and carrot sticks, or Southern Cheese Crackers (page 24), and it's great as a spread for sandwiches and wraps. The black-eyed peas replace the traditional chickpeas, giving the hummus a slightly darker color and fantastic nutty flavor.

1 In a blender or food processor, combine the lemon juice, tahini, and 2 tablespoons of the olive oil. Blend until smooth. Scrape down the sides of the container and add 1 cup of the black-eyed peas, the garlic, cumin, and salt. Blend until smooth, about 1 minute. Scrape down the sides and blend again for another minute. Add the remaining black-eyed peas and blend for about 20 seconds, or until the hummus has reached the creaminess you prefer. Transfer to a serving bowl and drizzle with the remaining olive oil.

2 The hummus will keep in an airtight container in the refrigerator for 1 week.

freezer friendly

Put the hummus in a sealable freezer bag and press out as much air as possible. Flatten the bag and freeze for up to 3 months. To use, thaw in the refrigerator overnight. You may need to add a drizzle of olive oil before serving to add moisture.

HOW TO
cook dried peas and beans

Preparing dried peas and beans, versus opting for canned, may take some extra time, but it's worth it. The texture is so much better! They are great for meals, for tossing into salads and soups, and for use in spreads like Black-Eyed Pea Hummus or dips like Southern Caviar (page 44). Here's how to do it:

SOAK. Rinse the peas or beans and discard any that do not look appealing. Put them in a large bowl, add 1½ tablespoons kosher salt, and soak uncovered overnight at room temperature.

COOK. Drain the peas or beans and transfer to a slow cooker. Add 1 teaspoon kosher salt and water to cover by 2 inches. Cook on low for 6 to 8 hours. Check for tenderness after 6 hours, and then again every 30 minutes, until they reach the desired tenderness. Alternatively, bring to a low simmer in a stockpot. Cook, adding water as needed, until fork-tender, 2 hours.

SERVE OR STORE. Add any desired seasonings and serve. Or let cool, transfer to airtight containers, and refrigerate for a week or freeze for up to 3 months.

WARM BRIE *with* HONEYED FRUIT COMPOTE

SERVES 12

¼ cup fresh orange juice

½ cup blueberries

½ cup blackberries

1 tablespoon grated orange zest

1 (8-ounce) wheel of Brie cheese

½ cup chopped walnuts

2 tablespoons honey

There is just something about warm, melty Brie that draws everyone's attention when you serve it. But when you top it with this honey fruit compote, you better believe it takes center stage! I love to use fruits that are in season, like berries during spring and summer and cranberries in fall and winter. You can easily substitute your favorite in-season fruit and make it your own. Serve with crackers or wedges of apples and pears.

1   Preheat the oven to 400°F.

2   In a 2-quart saucepan set over medium-low heat, simmer the orange juice until reduced, about 3 minutes. Add the blueberries, blackberries, and orange zest and cook until the mixture is thickened and coats the back of a spoon, about 5 more minutes.

3   Meanwhile, place the Brie on a 12-inch round ovenproof serving platter or in a medium ovenproof skillet. Bake until the cheese is softened, 12 to 15 minutes. Remove from the oven, top with the warm fruit mixture and the nuts, and drizzle honey on top. Serve immediately.

CRANBERRY WALNUT
Replace the blueberries and blackberries with 1 cup fresh cranberries. This version is quite festive during the holidays!

CRISPY CHICKEN WINGS

SERVES 8

3 tablespoons olive oil

1 teaspoon kosher salt

½ teaspoon freshly ground black pepper

½ teaspoon paprika

½ teaspoon ground cumin

¼ teaspoon cayenne pepper

2 garlic cloves, minced

3 tablespoons chopped onion

½ cup apple cider vinegar

6 pounds chicken wings, tips trimmed if preferred

Oil mister or cooking spray

My son, Sam, absolutely adores chicken wings, but I don't want to serve him deep-fried food all the time. So I ditched the deep-frying and found that cooking wings in the oven still resulted in a fantastic crispy texture—and the flavor is out of this world! If you are making these for a group of teenage guys, like I usually am, I recommend making extras. You'll thank me!

1   In a medium bowl, whisk together the olive oil, salt, black pepper, paprika, cumin, and cayenne. Add the garlic, onion, and vinegar and whisk to combine.

2   Place the chicken wings in a large plastic sealable bag. Pour the marinade over the chicken. Remove as much air as possible from the bag as you seal. Turn the bag from side to side to make sure the chicken is evenly coated. Place the bag flat on a small rimmed sheet pan (to catch any spills) and marinate in the refrigerator for 1 hour, or overnight for best results.

3   Preheat the oven to 425°F. Line a baking sheet with parchment paper or foil and lightly spray with oil.

4   Remove the chicken wings from the marinade and transfer them to the prepared baking sheet. Discard the marinade.

5   Bake until the chicken wings are cooked through and the skin is crispy, 50 to 55 minutes. Serve hot.

freezer friendly

Let the cooked wings cool completely. Transfer them to a sealable freezer bag and freeze for up to 3 months. To serve, place the frozen wings in a single layer on a rimmed baking sheet and bake at 350°F until heated through, about 30 minutes.

SOUTHERN CAVIAR

SERVES 12

2 cups cooked black-eyed peas (see sidebar, page 38)

2 cups cooked fresh or frozen and thawed corn kernels

2 medium fresh tomatoes, chopped

1 medium green bell pepper, chopped

½ medium Vidalia or other sweet onion, chopped

1 jalapeño pepper, or to taste, seeded and finely chopped

1 garlic clove, minced

1 teaspoon chopped fresh oregano or ½ teaspoon dried

1 teaspoon chopped fresh basil or ½ teaspoon dried

2 tablespoons olive oil

This spicy Southern twist on salsa features black-eyed peas and Vidalia onion. It's full of fresh ingredients, so you know it's good for you. You can add more jalapeño if you like a spicier spread, or use less if you prefer it milder. This recipe makes a gracious plenty, but it goes quickly! Serve it with Pecan Cheese Crackers (page 24), tortilla chips, or pita chips.

1 In a large bowl, combine the peas, corn, tomatoes, bell pepper, onion, jalapeño, garlic, oregano, basil, and oil.

2 To serve, use a slotted spoon to transfer the mixture to a serving bowl, discarding the excess liquid.

leftover makeover

SOUTHERN CAVIAR TOPPING
Though it's usually served as a dip, I also love to spoon this caviar on top of fish, chicken, salads, wraps, or even scrambled eggs. Talk about versatile!

SPINACH *and* ARTICHOKE–STUFFED MUSHROOMS

SERVES 10 TO 12

Oil mister or cooking spray

2 pounds (about 60) whole button mushrooms

1 tablespoon olive oil

10 ounces frozen artichoke hearts, thawed and chopped

5 ounces fresh spinach

1 garlic clove, minced

½ cup mayonnaise

½ cup plain whole-milk Greek yogurt

1 cup grated Parmesan cheese

I love just about anything with spinach and artichokes, and these stuffed mushrooms are one of my favorite ways to combine the two. Although technically this recipe makes enough for ten to twelve appetizer servings, I've found that folks really like to indulge in these little babies—they're always gone in a flash! It seems I'm not the only one who loves them.

1   Preheat the oven to 375°F. Lightly spray a baking sheet with oil.

2   Clean the mushrooms with a damp paper towel and carefully break off the stems. Chop the stems very finely; set aside. Arrange the mushroom caps on the prepared baking sheet with the cavity facing up.

3   In a 12-inch skillet set over medium heat, heat the olive oil. Add the chopped mushroom stems, the artichoke hearts, spinach, and garlic. Cook, stirring, until the spinach has wilted, 3 to 5 minutes. Remove the pan from the heat and stir in the mayonnaise, yogurt, and cheese. Spoon the mixture into the mushroom caps.

4   Bake until the mushrooms are hot and liquid is beginning to form under them, 15 minutes. Remove the pan from the oven and let cool for about 5 minutes before serving.

even easier!
Take these stuffed mushrooms from appetizer to entrée by using large mushroom caps instead. It makes a super-simple and delicious vegetarian dinner option where no one misses the meat!

southern hospitality
These mushrooms are like my little black dress for entertaining. I stuff the mushrooms, arrange them on a baking sheet, wrap tightly with plastic wrap, and refrigerate for up to 3 days. To serve, I remove the plastic wrap, bake, and transfer to a serving platter.

SKILLET SUPPERS

SUNDAY ROASTED CHICKEN

SERVES 6 TO 8

3½- to 5-pound
whole chicken

1 large bunch
fresh rosemary

1 large bunch
fresh thyme

3 tablespoons olive oil

1 teaspoon kosher salt

½ teaspoon freshly ground
black pepper

1 medium onion,
cut into quarters

3 large carrots, cut into
2-inch chunks

Sunday meals at my grandparents' house are some of my fondest memories. Grandmother was always sure to have one of each person's favorite dishes—peas for Daddy, green beans for my sister, fruit salad for Mama, deviled eggs for me, rolls for Granddaddy—and she'd alternate her desserts for each person from week to week. But one thing was always certain: We all loved her chicken! You don't have to save this recipe for Sunday; it's simple enough to make any night of the week special.

1   Preheat the oven to 425°F.

2   Remove the giblets from the chicken and discard. Pat the chicken dry with paper towels and place in a large ovenproof skillet. Put the rosemary and thyme in the chicken cavity. Tie the legs together with a piece of kitchen twine or string.

3   In a small bowl, combine the olive oil, salt, and pepper. Rub the mixture over the outside of the chicken. Arrange the onion and carrots around the chicken.

4   Roast until a thermometer inserted in the thickest part of the chicken registers 160°F and the juices run clear, 15 to 20 minutes per pound. Total cooking time will depend on the weight of the chicken. As a minimum, 50 minutes for a 3 ½-pound chicken and 1 hour 15 minutes for a 5 pound chicken. Let rest for 5 to 10 minutes. Baste the chicken, carrots, and onion with the pan juices. Serve in the skillet or transfer to a serving platter.

leftover makeover
Use any leftovers of this chicken for my Tarragon Chicken Salad (page 82).

SOUTHERN BUTTERMILK FRIED CHICKEN

SERVES 6 TO 8

3½- to 5-pound whole chicken, cut into pieces (or your choice of precut chicken breasts, thighs, and legs)

1 quart buttermilk

1 cup self-rising flour

2 teaspoons kosher salt

1 teaspoon freshly ground black pepper

½ teaspoon dried thyme

2 teaspoons hot sauce or ¼ teaspoon cayenne pepper

Peanut or canola oil, for frying

This is the fried chicken that I absolutely crave. It's crispy, juicy, and delicious! I came up with this method because I didn't want to drop my chicken in the deep fryer, submerging it completely in grease. So I found a solution that makes it a little lighter, and a lot less messy. After battering the chicken, I quickly brown it in a skillet and then bake it. Setting it on a wire rack for baking is key—this helps the chicken get amazingly crisp!

1   Put the chicken in a deep nonreactive pot or large glass bowl. Pour 3 cups of the buttermilk over the chicken, cover with plastic wrap, and refrigerate for at least 12 hours.

2   In a shallow dish, whisk together the flour, salt, pepper, and thyme. In a separate shallow dish, combine the remaining 1 cup buttermilk and the hot sauce.

3   Drain the chicken, discarding the buttermilk. Dip the chicken pieces in the buttermilk mixture first, then dredge in the flour mixture, shaking off any excess flour. Place the battered chicken on a plate and repeat with the remaining pieces. Let sit for about 5 minutes to help the batter adhere to the chicken.

4   Preheat the oven to 350°F. Set a wire rack over a rimmed baking sheet.

5   In a deep, heavy-bottomed cast-iron skillet set over medium heat, heat ½ to 1 inch of oil until it is 355°F to 360°F. Working in batches, add a few chicken pieces to the hot oil. Cook until lightly browned all over, 3 to 5 minutes per side. Using tongs, transfer the chicken to the wire rack. Repeat with the remaining chicken.

6   Bake until the chicken has cooked throughout and the juices run clear, 30 to 40 minutes.

NOTE Make sure your oil is between 355°F and 360°F to prevent the chicken from sticking to the pan.

(recipe continues)

make homemade buttermilk substitute

Don't have buttermilk on hand? Simply stir together 1 tablespoon distilled white vinegar or 1 tablespoon fresh lemon juice and 1 cup whole milk. Let sit for about 10 minutes to thicken.

leftover makeover

CHICKEN AND WAFFLES

Make a batch of buttermilk waffles by whisking together 2 cups all-purpose flour, ½ teaspoon kosher salt, 1½ tablespoons sugar, 1½ teaspoons baking powder, 1 teaspoon baking soda, 2 cups buttermilk, 2 large eggs, 4 tablespoons melted salted butter, and 1 teaspoon vanilla extract. Cook the waffles according to the waffle maker's instructions and top with fried chicken. Drizzle with maple syrup, sprinkle with Tabasco sauce, and serve! Makes about 6 (8-inch) round waffles or 10 to 12 (4-inch) square waffles.

southern hospitality

Pack a basket of fried chicken, Broccoli Pineapple Salad (page 162), Grandmother Earlene's Biscuits (page 174), Sweet Tea Concentrate (page 222), and a few slices of Mama's Cream Cheese Pound Cake (page 210) for a surprise supper anyone will love.

COFFEE-ENCRUSTED PRIME RIB

SERVES 6 TO 8

6-pound bone-in
standing rib roast
(about 2 servings per bone)

2 tablespoons kosher salt

2 tablespoons finely
ground coffee

1 teaspoon onion powder

1 teaspoon garlic powder

½ teaspoon freshly ground
black pepper

¼ teaspoon cayenne

This prime rib is perfect for special occasions and celebrations, like a family Christmas dinner. The best thing about this recipe? You prep it well in advance and then just roast it the day you plan to serve it. Note that the prime rib needs to be salted several days before cooking. When left on the meat for an extended period—at least one hour, and ideally four to five days—the salt seeps into the flesh and makes for a well-seasoned, juicy prime rib.

1 Ideally 4 to 5 days, but no less than 1 hour, before you plan to cook your prime rib, sprinkle the salt all over it. Wrap it tightly in plastic wrap and refrigerate.

2 An hour before cooking, remove the prime rib from the refrigerator, unwrap, and place it bone side down in a 12-inch ovenproof skillet. Let it sit for an hour to come to room temperature.

3 Meanwhile, in a small bowl, combine the coffee, onion powder, garlic powder, black pepper, and cayenne. Rub the mixture all over the meat.

4 Preheat the oven to 475°F for 30 minutes.

5 Roast the prime rib for 15 minutes. Reduce the temperature to 325°F and continue cooking until a thermometer inserted in the thickest part registers 130°F for medium rare, about 1½ hours (usually 15 minutes per pound), or to your desired doneness. Remove the prime rib from the oven, tent with foil, and let rest for 20 minutes before slicing and serving.

leftover makeover

PRIME RIB SANDWICHES
Serve thin slices of leftover prime rib on Boots Butler's Yeast Rolls (page 182) that have been split in half and slathered with Dijon mustard and mayonnaise.

PEPPER JELLY PORK MEDALLIONS

SERVES 6 TO 8

1 tablespoon olive oil

2 (12-ounce) pork tenderloins, cut into 1-inch-thick slices

¾ cup Pepper Jelly (page 220)

Pepper jelly has always been a staple in my family's pantry. I share our family recipe on page 220 and am practically begging you to make it, if for no other reason than trying this quick and simple recipe for pork medallions. It's a meal my whole family can't get enough of! Little do they know that cooking just couldn't get much simpler.

1   Preheat the oven to 350°F.

2   In a medium ovenproof skillet set over medium heat, heat the olive oil. Add the pork medallions and sear until browned, 3 to 5 minutes per side. Transfer the skillet to the oven and bake until the meat is no longer pink in the center, 15 to 20 minutes.

3   Remove the pan from the oven, spoon the pepper jelly over the pork, and tent with foil or parchment paper. Let rest for 5 minutes before serving.

leftover makeover

TOASTED PORK SANDWICHES
Spread slices of Cuban or sourdough bread with Dijon mustard, layer on the leftover pork medallions, and top with Swiss cheese. Toast the sandwich in a cast-iron skillet over high heat. Serve right away!

ROASTED VENISON FILLETS

SERVES 6

1 venison backstrap
(about 2½ pounds)

1 quart buttermilk,
or as needed

3 tablespoons Espresso
Chili Spice Blend (page 227)

2 tablespoons chopped
fresh rosemary

1 tablespoon olive oil

2 tablespoons salted butter

½ cup beef broth

leftover makeover

VENISON BISCUITS
Yes, you can eat leftover
venison the next day! I
smear a little butter on
halved biscuits (page 174)
and toast them in a 425°F
oven until golden brown,
about 10 minutes. Then
I serve them with slivers
of venison and some blue
cheese crumbles, chopped
fresh rosemary, and a pinch
of kosher salt.

I always loved going hunting and fishing with my daddy when growing up. Those hours spent together were special—especially since I chatted away the entire time. Needless to say, the freezer wasn't stocked because of my contributions, but we enjoyed ourselves immensely. Thankfully, my brother-in-law Steve and my son, Sam, have taken up the hunting reins, and I still get to cook with very fresh deer meat. This roasted venison recipe uses the backstrap—the most highly regarded cut of venison in my daddy's book—making it perfect for special occasions. If venison isn't available, you can use roast or beef tenderloin instead.

1   Put the venison in a nonreactive bowl or casserole dish. Pour in enough buttermilk to cover by about 1 inch. Cover tightly with plastic wrap and refrigerate overnight.

2   Preheat the oven to 450°F.

3   Pour off the buttermilk and discard. Let the venison sit until it reaches room temperature, about 20 minutes.

4   Meanwhile, in a small bowl, combine the spice blend and 1 tablespoon of the rosemary. Rub the mixture onto the venison.

5   In a medium skillet set over medium heat, heat the olive oil. Add the venison and cook until browned on both sides, 3 to 5 minutes per side. Transfer the skillet to the middle rack of the oven.

6   Roast until a thermometer inserted in the thickest part of the meat registers 125°F, 15 to 18 minutes. Transfer the venison to a plate.

7   Set the same skillet, with all of the drippings, over medium heat. Add the butter, beef broth, and remaining tablespoon rosemary and cook, using a wooden spoon to scrape up the browned bits on the bottom of the skillet, until the sauce has thickened and reduced by about half, around 5 minutes. Remove the pan from the heat.

8   Cut the venison into ¼- to ½-inch slices and serve with sauce spooned over the top.

SWEET-AND-SOUR MEATBALLS *with* ZUCCHINI

SERVES 6 TO 8

meatballs

2 pounds lean ground beef

½ medium onion, chopped

1 garlic clove, minced

¼ cup Applesauce (recipe follows)

1 tablespoon Worcestershire sauce

sauce

½ medium onion, chopped

1 small green bell pepper, chopped

3 cups tomato sauce, homemade (page 229) or store-bought

¼ cup Applesauce (recipe follows)

1 tablespoon fresh lemon juice

1 garlic clove, minced

½ teaspoon kosher salt

5 medium zucchini, shaved into thin strips with a vegetable peeler

Grated or shaved Parmesan cheese, for garnish

Mama's sweet-and-sour meatballs were legendary at our house when I was growing up. Whenever she made them, there was no need to ask us to come to the table more than once. Now that I cook them for my own family, I see why she loved making them as much as we loved eating them—talk about simple! These meatballs are delicious any way that you serve them, but I especially love them over a bed of shaved zucchini, which is much lighter than pasta (and adds some veggies!).

1   **Make the meatballs:** In a large bowl, combine the ground beef, onion, garlic, applesauce, and Worcestershire sauce. Using a tablespoon measure or a spoon, shape the mixture into 2-inch meatballs.

2   In a 12-inch skillet set over medium heat, working in batches, cook the meatballs, turning occasionally to ensure that all sides brown, about 7 minutes. Using a slotted spoon, transfer the meatballs to large bowl. Discard any drippings left in the pan.

3   **Make the sauce:** In the same skillet, set over medium heat, combine the onion and bell pepper. Cook, stirring, until tender, about 3 minutes. Add the tomato sauce, applesauce, lemon juice, garlic, and salt and cook until the sauce has reduced and thickened, about 20 minutes. Add the meatballs to the sauce and simmer for 10 minutes.

4   Serve over the zucchini strips, sprinkled with the Parmesan.

leftover makeover

SWEET-AND-SOUR MEATBALL ROLLS

Reheat leftover meatballs and sauce in a medium saucepan over medium heat. Spoon the meatballs and sauce into yeast rolls (page 182) for a delicious sandwich.

(recipe continues)

freezer friendly

Cook a few batches of meatballs, let them cool completely, arrange on a rimmed baking sheet, and flash freeze for 15 minutes. Then transfer to freezer bags and store in the freezer for up to 3 months. For a quick weeknight meal, thaw in the refrigerator overnight and reheat in a saucepan over medium heat in the sauce or a tablespoon of olive oil.

APPLESAUCE

MAKES 6 CUPS

3 large sweet apples, such as Honeycrisp or Macintosh, peeled and cored

3 Granny Smith apples, peeled and cored

½ cup water, apple juice, or apple cider

Cut the apples into wedges and put them in a large saucepan. Add the water, set the pot over low heat, and bring to a simmer. Cook until the apples are easily mashed with the back of a spoon, about 30 minutes. Remove the pan from the heat. Working in batches, process the apples in a food processor or blender until the sauce reaches the consistency you prefer. The applesauce will keep in an airtight container in the refrigerator for up to 3 weeks or in the freezer for a year.

SAM'S OVEN-FRIED HALIBUT

SERVES 6

6 (6-ounce) halibut fillets

2 teaspoons olive oil

½ cup buttermilk

½ cup Bread Crumbs (recipe follows) or store-bought plain bread crumbs seasoned with a pinch of salt and pepper

2 teaspoons Stone House Seasoning (page 226)

1 teaspoon paprika

1 tablespoon salted butter, melted

Years ago, Bart went on a fishing trip to Alaska with his father and brothers. He called with good news that he'd caught a huge halibut and asked if I'd get the freezer ready to hold it all. I think we ate more halibut in that year than we'd eaten in our whole lives, but boy did we love it! This is the recipe that I made most often during that year and one that I continue to make routinely. It's one of Sam's favorites!

1 Preheat the oven to 475°F. Drizzle the olive oil into a large ovenproof skillet, tilting to make sure a thin layer of oil coats the bottom of the skillet and set aside.

2 Pour the buttermilk into a shallow dish. In another shallow dish, stir together the bread crumbs, seasoning mix, and paprika. Dip each fillet in the buttermilk and then dredge in the bread crumb mixture, coating both sides. Place the halibut in the prepared skillet and drizzle with the melted butter.

3 Bake until the halibut is cooked through and flakes easily with a fork, 10 to 12 minutes.

BREAD CRUMBS

MAKES ABOUT 4 CUPS

½-pound loaf of day-old bread, cut into 2-inch pieces

½ teaspoon kosher salt

½ teaspoon freshly ground black pepper

1 Preheat the oven to 300°F.

2 Place the bread, salt, and pepper in a food processor or large blender and pulse until fine crumbs are formed. Pour the crumbs onto a rimmed baking sheet in a single layer, using additional pans if needed.

3 Bake until the crumbs begin to turn golden, about 5 minutes. Remove the pan from the oven and let cool for 10 to 15 minutes. The bread crumbs will keep in an airtight container at room temperature for up to 2 weeks, or in the freezer for a few months.

leftover makeover

QUICK AND EASY FISH TACOS

Heat 1 tablespoon olive oil in a medium skillet set over medium heat until it shimmers. Add a medium flour or corn tortilla and cook until golden on each side, about 1 minute per side. Transfer to a plate and top with a piece of leftover halibut, some shredded cabbage, and a little Southern Caviar (page 44) for a fish taco in a flash!

EASY BLACKENED CATFISH

SERVES 6

6 (6-ounce) catfish fillets

¼ cup Blackening Seasoning, or more to taste (page 226)

1 tablespoon olive oil

Creamy Grits (page 72)

1 lemon, cut into wedges, for serving

When I was growing up, my family spent summer weekends on Lake Martin in Alabama, where I loved to be the first up in the mornings to fish with Daddy while the lake was calm and the bitin' was good. Daddy would just about always bait my hook for catfish. I'm not sure if this was because it was an easy one to catch or because I'd squeal every time I caught the bewhiskered fish. Now when my family goes fishing at the lake, I try to keep a bit more composure. This catfish recipe is fast and fabulous! If catfish isn't available, any mild white fish will do.

1   Dry the fish fillets with a paper towel and sprinkle both sides with the blackening seasoning.

2   In a large skillet set over medium heat, heat the oil until it begins to shimmer slightly. Carefully add the fillets to the skillet and cook until browned on one side, 3 to 5 minutes. Flip and cook the other side until the fish is dark, crisp, easily flakes with a fork, and is cooked through, 3 to 5 more minutes. Serve over the grits with lemon wedges on the side.

leftover makeover

BLACKENED CATFISH PO-BOYS
Split a loaf of French bread and spread with a bit of mayonnaise. Layer the blackened catfish, lettuce, tomato, and pickles on one half, top with the other half, cut into quarters, and dig in!

southern hospitality
There's nothing like a fish supper in the summertime after a lucky fishing trip! Invite friends and family over for a fun meal of Blackened Catfish, Heirloom Tomato Salad with Charred Corn and Okra (page 166), Georgia Peach Crisp (page 208), and Sweet Tea Concentrate (page 222).

BROILED GROUPER *with* LEMON BASIL BUTTER

SERVES 6

1 tablespoon olive oil

2 pounds grouper fillets

2 tablespoons salted butter, at room temperature

1 tablespoon chopped fresh basil

1 teaspoon grated lemon zest

⅛ teaspoon kosher salt

⅛ teaspoon freshly ground black pepper

My family loves fish—so much so that we could happily eat it time and time again and never get tired of it. This broiled grouper is especially a hit on those weeknights when I am short on time to get supper on the table. Served with a green salad, this is a restaurant-quality meal without the wait!

1 Preheat the broiler.

2 Coat the bottom of a large skillet with olive oil. Place the grouper into the skillet and broil about 8 inches from the heat until the fish is lightly browned and easily flakes with a fork, about 10 minutes.

3 Meanwhile, stir together the butter, basil, lemon zest, salt, and pepper.

4 Remove the fish from the oven, divide the lemon basil butter among the fillets, and serve.

leftover makeover

BROILED GROUPER PASTA
Top cooked pasta—or even shaved zucchini ribbons—with leftover reheated grouper and a squeeze of fresh lemon juice.

CREAMY ARTICHOKE CHICKEN

SERVES 6

2 tablespoons olive oil

6 boneless, skinless chicken breasts

½ pound fresh mushrooms, sliced

2 tablespoons salted butter

2 tablespoons all-purpose flour

1 cup chicken stock, homemade (page 104) or store-bought

1 cup heavy cream

1 teaspoon Stone House Seasoning (page 226)

1 (9-ounce) package frozen artichoke hearts, thawed, drained, and quartered

½ cup freshly grated Parmesan cheese

This rich, heartwarming casserole is made with chicken, mushrooms, and artichokes, all nestled into a flavorful homemade sauce and topped with Parmesan cheese. It is creamy, dreamy, and oh-so-delicious!

1   Preheat the oven to 350°F.

2   In a 12-inch ovenproof skillet set over medium-high heat, heat 1½ tablespoons of the olive oil. Add the chicken breasts and cook until well browned on both sides, about 8 minutes per side. Transfer to a platter.

3   In the same skillet set over medium heat, add the remaining ½ tablespoon olive oil. Add the mushrooms and cook, stirring, until browned, about 5 minutes. Using a slotted spoon, transfer to a small bowl.

4   In the same skillet set over medium-high heat, melt the butter. Whisk in the flour until smooth. Cook, whisking constantly, until the mixture begins to bubble, about 5 minutes. Whisk in the chicken stock and cream. Reduce the heat to medium-low and cook, whisking constantly, until the sauce begins to boil and thicken, about 10 minutes. Remove the pan from the heat and stir in the seasoning mix. Add the cooked mushrooms, artichoke hearts, and Parmesan cheese and stir well. Nestle the chicken into the sauce and vegetables, and spoon the sauce over the chicken.

5   Bake until the chicken is cooked through and the juices run clear when the chicken is pricked with a sharp knife, about 30 minutes. Serve immediately.

leftover makeover

CREAMY ARTICHOKE PASTA
Reheat leftover artichoke chicken and spoon it over cooked pasta. Top with shaved Parmesan and serve.

CITRUS SHRIMP

SERVES 6

1 tablespoon olive oil

1 cup fresh orange juice

½ cup fresh lemon juice

3 garlic cloves, minced

1 tablespoon finely chopped onion

1 tablespoon chopped fresh parsley

½ teaspoon freshly ground black pepper

3 pounds medium shrimp, peeled and deveined

1 medium orange, cut into wedges

1 medium lemon, cut into wedges

Although my family spent most weekends on Lake Martin, at least one week of the year was reserved for the beach. We'd pack Mama's car to the gills and head out well before daybreak so that we'd arrive in plenty of time for supper, since we knew Daddy would cook fresh Gulf shrimp. This citrus shrimp recipe takes me right back to those trips. Bright and fresh from the citrus, it's fast enough for a weeknight meal and pretty enough for entertaining, especially when served on a platter with lemon and orange wedges.

1   In a medium bowl, whisk together the olive oil, orange juice, lemon juice, garlic, onion, 2 teaspoons of the parsley, and pepper. Pour the mixture into a large skillet set over medium heat. Bring to a simmer and cook until reduced by half, 5 to 8 minutes. Add the shrimp, cover, and cook until they turn pink, about 5 minutes. Top with the remaining parsley.

2   Serve with the orange and lemon wedges on the side.

leftover makeover

CITRUS SHRIMP AND AVOCADO SALAD

If you have any shrimp left over, toss them with about 2 tablespoons finely chopped red onion and 2 chopped avocados, and serve on a bed of mixed lettuce greens. Make a vinaigrette by whisking together ¼ cup olive oil, ¼ cup red wine vinegar, 1 teaspoon Dijon mustard, and ½ teaspoon Stone House Seasoning (page 226) and serve with the salad. Makes about ½ cup vinaigrette.

CREOLE SHRIMP *and* GRITS

SERVES 6

2 tablespoons olive oil

1 medium onion, chopped

1 cup chopped celery

6 medium plum tomatoes, chopped

1 green bell pepper, cored, seeded, and chopped

1 garlic clove, minced

2 tablespoons Worcestershire sauce

1 teaspoon chili powder

1 teaspoon kosher salt

½ teaspoon freshly ground black pepper

1½ pounds medium shrimp, peeled and deveined

Creamy Grits (at right)

Shrimp and grits is about as iconic a dish as you can find in the South—and it seems that there are almost as many recipes as there are people making it! Though I've rarely tried a version that I didn't like, this one has stolen my heart, lock, stock, and barrel. It makes a regular appearance at our house during shrimp season, but you can also use frozen shrimp, as long as it is thawed and well drained. For the grits, you can use quick-cooking white or yellow grits, or use my simple slow-cooker method for stone-ground grits (see sidebar).

1   In a medium skillet set over medium heat, heat the olive oil. Add the onion and celery and cook, stirring, until tender but not browned, about 3 minutes. Add the tomatoes, bell pepper, garlic, Worcestershire sauce, chili powder, salt, and pepper and cook, stirring, for 5 more minutes. Add the shrimp. Cover and cook until the shrimp are opaque and cooked through, 5 minutes.

2   Divide the grits among serving dishes. Spoon the shrimp over the grits and drizzle with the pan sauce.

CREAMY GRITS

MAKES ABOUT 6 CUPS

6 cups water or chicken stock, homemade (page 104) or store-bought

1½ teaspoons kosher salt

1½ cups quick-cooking grits

¼ cup freshly grated Parmesan cheese

In a large saucepan set over medium-high heat, bring the water and salt to a boil. While whisking constantly, slowly pour the grits into the boiling water. Reduce the heat to low and simmer, whisking often, until the grits become thick and creamy, about 5 minutes. Remove the pan from the heat, stir in the cheese, and serve.

cook grits
in a slow cooker

It's very easy to cook grits in
a slow cooker, but make sure
you use stone-ground grits,
not the quick-cooking kind.
Put the grits in a medium bowl
and cover with water. Let soak
for about 10 minutes. Scoop
off bits of kernel that float to
the top of the water, and
then drain. Combine all of
the ingredients in the slow
cooker, whisk together,
cover, and cook on low
for 3 hours. Voilà!

EASY SKILLET LASAGNA

SERVES 6 TO 8

1 tablespoon olive oil

½ medium onion, chopped

1½ pounds ground beef

1 teaspoon Stone House Seasoning (page 226)

1 teaspoon chopped fresh oregano or ½ teaspoon dried

⅛ teaspoon red pepper flakes

4 cups tomato sauce, homemade (page 229) or store-bought

8 lasagna noodles, broken into 2-inch pieces

¾ cup freshly grated Parmesan cheese

½ cup ricotta cheese

Lasagna has always been one of Sam's favorite meals. Since the dish can take quite a lot of work (and time) to put together, I make a version that comes together in a jiffy. This skillet lasagna is ready in thirty minutes—no kidding! If you have a teenage son like I do, I can't recommend it enough!

1   In a medium skillet set over medium heat, heat the olive oil. Add the onion and cook, stirring, until translucent, about 3 minutes. Add the ground beef and cook, breaking up the meat with a wooden spoon, until browned through, about 5 minutes. Pour off any excess fat.

2   Return the pan to medium heat and stir in the seasoning mix, oregano, red pepper flakes, tomato sauce, and noodle pieces. Bring to a boil and then reduce the heat to medium-low. Simmer, cover, and cook until the noodles are tender, 18 to 20 minutes.

3   Remove the pan from the heat and stir in ½ cup of the Parmesan cheese. Top with dollops of the ricotta cheese and the remaining ¼ cup Parmesan, and serve.

leftover makeover

MEATY CHEESY BREAD

Preheat the oven to 425°F. Slice a loaf of French bread in half lengthwise. Brush the bread with 1 tablespoon olive oil mixed with ½ teaspoon Stone House Seasoning (page 226). Toast the bread until golden brown, about 10 minutes. Ladle on leftover lasagna and top with about ¼ cup grated Parmesan cheese. Return to the oven and bake until the cheese has melted, 8 to 10 minutes.

freezer friendly

Portion the cooked, cooled lasagna into ovenproof freezer containers and press plastic wrap onto the surface of the food. Wrap the containers well with foil. Label and store in the freezer for up to 3 months. To serve, thaw in the refrigerator overnight. Remove the foil and plastic wrap from the container and re-cover with the foil. Bake at 325°F until heated through, 15 to 20 minutes.

SLOW COOKER SUPPERS

POT ROAST *with* ROOT VEGETABLES

SERVES 8

1 pound carrots, cut into 2-inch pieces

3 large russet potatoes, peeled and cut into 2-inch pieces

3 parsnips, peeled and cut into 2-inch pieces

2 medium onions, cut into wedges

4 celery stalks, cut into 2-inch pieces

5-pound beef roast (chuck, shoulder, or round)

2 tablespoons Worcestershire sauce

1 teaspoon Stone House Seasoning (page 226)

3 sprigs of fresh thyme or ½ teaspoon dried

This classic dish is always a favorite with my family. I made this pot roast every single week when I had an office job, and my family never tired of it! It is so simple to toss everything into the slow cooker, set the timer, and come home to a warm, delicious supper. When I decided to stay home with our son, I realized that I was working just as hard as I ever had in an office. So I still turn to those tried-and-true recipes that became a staple earlier in our marriage, like this one! This recipe makes a gracious plenty, practically guaranteeing you'll have enough for leftovers.

1　Arrange the carrots, potatoes, parsnips, onions, and celery in the bottom of a 6-quart slow cooker. Place the roast on top of the vegetables and sprinkle evenly with the Worcestershire sauce, seasoning mix, and thyme.

2　Cover and cook on low until the roast easily pulls apart with two forks, for 6 to 8 hours.

3　Thinly slice or pull the roast into large pieces and arrange the vegetables on the side. Drizzle the juices over everything and serve.

leftover makeover

POT ROAST POT PIE

Make the dough for Grandmother Earlene's Biscuits (page 174). Chop the pot roast into bite-sized pieces and arrange the pot roast, vegetables, and sauce in a casserole dish. Dollop the biscuit batter over the top. Bake in a 475°F oven until the biscuits are golden brown and the pot pie is heated through, about 12 minutes.

freezer friendly

Portion the cooked pot roast into sealable freezer bags, removing as much air as possible as you seal. Press the bag flat and freeze for up to 3 months. To serve, thaw in the refrigerator overnight. Reheat in a medium saucepan set over medium heat until warmed through, 15 to 20 minutes.

BRAISED BEEF SHORT RIBS

SERVES 6

7 beef short ribs, bone-in

1 medium onion, quartered

5 carrots, sliced

3 celery stalks, sliced

2 cups beef broth

2 sprigs of fresh thyme

2 sprigs of fresh rosemary

2 bay leaves

Kosher salt and freshly ground black pepper

Rich and hearty, short ribs are one of my favorite things to cook when cooler weather calls for comfort food. Traditionally, short ribs get a dusting of flour before being seared in oil and cooked low and slow in the oven. I wanted a much easier way to cook this dish for my family, so my recipe skips those first steps. Instead, the short ribs cook in the slow cooker until they are falling off the bone; then I roast them briefly to give them a flavorful crust.

1   Arrange the short ribs in a 6-quart slow cooker. Add the onion, carrots, celery, and beef broth. Nestle the thyme, rosemary, and bay leaves into the liquid. Season with salt and pepper. Cover and cook on low for 8 hours.

2   Preheat the oven to 450°F.

3   Remove the thyme, rosemary, and bay leaves and discard. Using tongs, carefully transfer the short ribs to a large roasting pan, leaving the vegetables in the slow cooker. Roast the short ribs until browned, 15 to 20 minutes. Remove from the oven and let rest for 5 minutes. You can serve the ribs on the bone or shred the meat and discard the bones.

4   While the ribs are roasting, skim the fat from the drippings in the slow cooker. Pour the drippings into a medium saucepan set over medium heat. Cook until the liquid has reduced by half, about 30 minutes. Spoon the sauce over the short ribs and vegetables and serve with additional sauce on the side.

leftover makeover

SHORT RIB TACOS

Shred the meat (about 1 pound) from the bones and discard the bones. Put the meat and any reserved sauce in a saucepan set over medium heat. For about 8 tacos, add ½ teaspoon each cayenne pepper, cumin, and garlic powder and cook until heated through, about 12 minutes. Put the meat in taco shells and top with diced avocado and chopped cilantro.

freezer friendly

Let the cooked short ribs cool completely. Freeze the short ribs in airtight containers for up to 3 months. To reheat, thaw in the refrigerator overnight. Warm the short ribs in a 350°F oven until heated through, about 20 minutes.

PERFECT PORK ROAST

SERVES 8 TO 10

3-pound pork shoulder
blade roast or picnic roast

2 tablespoons
Worcestershire sauce

3 tablespoons Dry Rub Mix
(page 227)

One thing I was taught growing up is that simple is usually best. Life can be complicated enough without making things harder than they need to be. That lesson holds true for so many things in life, from raising a family to cooking for them. Take this pork roast, for instance—I could add all sorts of elaborate things or spend time fiddling with it, but here's what works: Spend about five minutes early in the morning to combine the ingredients, cook it low and slow, and don't fuss. That's it!

1   Place the meat in a 6-quart slow cooker. Pour the Worcestershire sauce over the pork and sprinkle with the dry rub. Cover and cook on low for 8 to 10 hours. Set the slow cooker to the warm setting and leave the meat for about 4 more hours, or until it easily pulls apart with two forks.

2   Transfer the meat to a cutting board and let rest for 5 to 10 minutes. Slice or pull the meat, and baste with the juices in the slow cooker before serving.

leftover makeover

PULLED PORK SANDWICHES

Slather the pork in your favorite barbecue sauce (or try my homemade sauce, page 217) and pile it on hamburger buns or Boots Butler's Yeast Rolls (page 182). Top with your favorite condiments—my family loves pickles and coleslaw, but a spoonful of Chow Chow (page 230) is a close second!

freezer friendly

Let the cooked pork cool completely. Portion into sealable freezer bags, removing as much air as possible. Freeze for up to 3 months. To serve, thaw in the refrigerator overnight. Tent with foil and reheat in a 350°F oven until warmed through, 20 to 30 minutes.

TARRAGON CHICKEN SALAD

SERVES 6

Oil mister or cooking spray

1 pound boneless, skinless chicken breasts

½ cup chopped celery

1 cup red or white grapes, halved

½ cup chopped pecans, toasted (see Tip)

1 cup mayonnaise

1 teaspoon kosher salt

½ teaspoon freshly ground black pepper

1 tablespoon chopped fresh tarragon

If I made just one thing for Bart for the rest of his life, it would be this chicken salad. It is hands down his number one requested meal for supper during warmer months, and he could eat it for lunch at least three days a week without complaint! There are a million recipes for chicken salad, but this is my favorite. The celery and toasted pecans add a nice crunch, while the grapes lend a hint of sweetness. And the fresh, herbal tarragon brings the flavor up a notch. While delicious on its own, it is also perfect in sandwiches and wraps or on a bed of lettuce.

1   Lightly spray a 6-quart slow cooker with oil. Arrange the chicken in the slow cooker, cover, and cook on high for 4 hours.

2   Remove the chicken from the slow cooker, reserving any drippings for another use or discard, and cut into ½-inch cubes. Transfer to a large bowl. Add the celery, grapes, and pecans.

3   In a 2-cup measure or small bowl, combine the mayonnaise, salt, and pepper. Stir the mixture into the chicken. Gently fold in the tarragon. Serve immediately or store in an airtight container in the refrigerator for up to 3 days.

lightened up

Replace all of the mayonnaise in the dressing with Greek yogurt for a lighter version that tastes just as good.

HOW TO

toast pecans

Preheat the oven to 300°F. Spread the pecans evenly on a rimmed baking sheet. Bake until browned and fragrant, stirring halfway through, about 10 minutes. Let cool.

BRISKET *with* TOMATO GRAVY

SERVES 6 TO 8

2½- to 3-pound brisket

5 medium potatoes, peeled and cut into quarters

1 small onion, sliced

4 medium tomatoes, peeled, seeded, and chopped

1 tablespoon packed dark brown sugar

1½ teaspoons freshly ground black pepper

1½ teaspoons kosher salt

1 cup chicken stock, homemade (page 104) or store-bought

1 cup tomato sauce, homemade (page 228) or store-bought

1 tablespoon cornstarch (optional)

People usually think that Southern brisket has to be smoked all day and then slathered with barbecue sauce. But I think instead of this recipe, which I made when Bart and I were first married. I wanted to make it extra special and had the butcher help me pick out the perfect cut. I made sure that every ingredient was just right as I added them to the slow cooker in the morning before I left for work, and then looked forward to it all day. That night, I rushed in the door at the same time as Bart, gave him a sassy little smile, and said, "Just you wait for supper! You are going to love me even more!" My heart sank as I walked into the kitchen and saw the electrical cord neatly wound around the cooker, which was cold as ice. Thankfully, I can laugh now, looking back on it, especially since I've now made this brisket—successfully—many times!

1   Put the brisket in a 6-quart slow cooker. Add the potatoes, onion, and tomatoes.

2   In a small bowl, combine the brown sugar, pepper, salt, chicken stock, and ½ cup of the tomato sauce and pour the mixture over the brisket.

3   Cover and cook on low for 8 hours, or until the meat is fork-tender. Transfer the meat and potatoes to a platter and let rest.

4   Pour the liquid from the slow cooker into a medium saucepan set over medium-high heat. Add the remaining ½ cup tomato sauce and cook until reduced by half, about 10 minutes. If you'd like a thicker gravy, whisk the cornstarch with ¼ cup cold water until smooth; then, whisking constantly, pour into the gravy and continue whisking over the heat for a minute or two to let the gravy thicken. Pour the tomato gravy over the brisket and vegetables, slice, and serve.

freezer friendly

Portion the brisket, vegetables, and gravy equally into sealable freezer bags, removing as much air as possible as you seal. Press flat and freeze for up to 3 months. To serve, thaw in the refrigerator overnight. Reheat in a medium saucepan set over medium heat until warmed through, 15 to 20 minutes.

STICKY MOLASSES BBQ RIBS

SERVES 6

Oil mister or cooking spray

3 to 4 pounds ribs,
cut into individual ribs

barbecue sauce

1 cup ketchup

½ cup molasses

2 tablespoons apple
cider vinegar

½ teaspoon hot sauce

2 teaspoons chili powder

1 teaspoon garlic powder

1 teaspoon kosher salt

1 teaspoon freshly ground
black pepper

I have a confession. I prefer these ribs over those cooked on the smoker or grill any day of the week! There. I said it. The slow, moist heat of the slow cooker just works magic on ribs, making them fall-off-the-bone, finger-licking delicious! Not to mention, they're a whole lot less work, since you don't have to check on them constantly. You no longer need to fire up the grill the next time you have ribs on the menu.

1   Lightly spray a 6-quart slow cooker with oil and add the ribs.

2   **Make the barbecue sauce:** In a small bowl, whisk together the ketchup, molasses, vinegar, hot sauce, chili powder, garlic powder, salt, and pepper. Pour half of the sauce over the ribs and refrigerate the remaining sauce while the ribs cook.

3   Cover the ribs and cook on low for 8 hours. Pour the remaining sauce over the ribs and remove from the slow cooker. Serve immediately.

leftover makeover

BARBECUE NACHOS

Preheat the oven to 475°F. Scatter tortilla chips in a single layer on a baking sheet. Remove the meat from the bones and pile on top of the tortilla chips. Top with chopped jalapeños, tomatoes, red onion, beans, and a bit of the leftover barbecue sauce. Bake until the meat is warmed through, about 10 minutes. Top with shredded Monterey Jack cheese and bake until the cheese melts, about 3 more minutes. Serve with chopped avocado.

freezer friendly

Let the cooked ribs cool. Place them in a single layer on a parchment paper–lined rimmed baking sheet and cover with plastic wrap. Flash freeze until completely frozen, about 30 minutes. Transfer to sealable freezer bags, removing as much air as possible as you seal. Freeze for 3 months. To serve, thaw in the refrigerator overnight. Tent with foil and reheat in a 325°F oven until warmed through, about 30 minutes.

SPICY SLOW COOKER CHICKEN SLIDERS

SERVES 6

Oil mister or cooking spray

4 to 6 boneless, skinless
chicken breasts

Sweet and Spicy BBQ sauce
(page 217)

6 yeast rolls, homemade
(page 182) or store-bought

Dill pickles, homemade
(page 218) or store-bought,
for serving

If you are looking for a quick and easy weeknight staple, this recipe is for you! It's as easy as tossing the chicken into the slow cooker and pouring in the barbecue sauce—the slow cooker does all the work. Simply shred the cooked chicken with two forks. To serve, pile it onto yeast rolls with an extra bit of barbecue sauce. Then top it off with dill pickles. It's that easy!

1   Lightly spray the inside of a 6-quart slow cooker with oil. Put the chicken in the cooker and pour half of the barbecue sauce over the top.

2   Cover and cook on low for 6 hours. Shred the chicken with two forks.

3   Serve on yeast rolls with the remaining sauce and pickles.

leftover makeover

STUFFED SWEET POTATOES

Scrub the sweet potatoes clean, coat their skins with a bit of olive oil, and sprinkle with a pinch of salt. Wrap each potato in parchment paper or foil and cook in a slow cooker on low for 6 to 8 hours. Unwrap the potatoes, split them open, and stuff them with leftover barbecue sauce and shredded chicken. Simply scrumptious!

BALSAMIC BEEF

SERVES 6 TO 8

3- to 4-pound boneless chuck or round roast

1 cup beef broth

½ cup balsamic vinegar

1 tablespoon Worcestershire sauce

1 tablespoon soy sauce

1 tablespoon honey

4 garlic cloves, chopped

½ teaspoon red pepper flakes

This very flavorful roast beef takes only five minutes of hands-on time to prepare—I promise! I often cook two at once so that I have plenty of leftovers throughout the week. On the first day, we love it served with Green Beans with New Potatoes (page 128), Roasted Okra (page 136), and Popovers (page 184). The next day, we pile the beef into hoagies or sub rolls and serve the sauce on the side for kid-friendly French dip sandwiches. And then, we use the leftovers as a stuffing for mushroom caps (see below). I'm sure you'll find your own favorite remakes!

1 Lightly spray the inside of a 6-quart slow cooker with oil. Put the beef in the slow cooker.

2 In a 2-cup measure or a small bowl, combine the broth, vinegar, Worcestershire sauce, soy sauce, honey, garlic, and red pepper flakes. Pour the mixture over the beef.

3 Cover and cook on high for 4 hours or low for 6 to 8 hours.

4 Using tongs, transfer the roast beef to a serving dish. Break it apart slightly with two forks, and then ladle ¼ to ½ cup of the sauce in the slow cooker over the beef for serving. Refrigerate the remaining sauce in an airtight container for another use.

leftover makeover
STUFFED MUSHROOMS
Preheat the oven to 350°F. Arrange 8 medium to large portobello mushroom caps on a large baking sheet. Skim any fat from the sauce and discard. Pour ½ cup of the sauce into a saucepan set over medium heat. Stir in 1 tablespoon butter and some leftover beef and cook until warmed through, about 8 minutes. Fill each mushroom cap with beef and drizzle with sauce. Bake until the mushrooms have softened, 15 to 20 minutes.

freezer friendly
Portion into sealable freezer bags, removing as much air as possible as you seal. Press flat and freeze for up to 3 months. To reheat, thaw in the refrigerator overnight. Tent with foil and reheat in a 350°F oven until warmed through, 20 to 30 minutes.

cook perfect fluffy rice

Rinse 2 cups long-grain white rice in cold water. Drain well. Put the rice in a medium saucepan with 2 cups water and ½ teaspoon kosher salt. Bring to a boil over medium heat and then immediately reduce the heat to low. Cover with a tight-fitting lid and cook at a low simmer until all of the water has been absorbed, 10 to 12 minutes. Fluff the rice before serving. While this recipe yields 6 cups of cooked rice, you can adjust if more or less is needed. Use the rule of thumb that ⅓ cup of uncooked rice will yield about 1 cup of cooked rice.

EASY PEPPER STEAK

SERVES 6 TO 8

2 pounds beef round steak, cut into strips

2 tablespoons Worcestershire sauce

2 tablespoons all-purpose flour

1 tablespoon paprika

2 teaspoons Stone House Seasoning (page 226)

½ medium onion, cut into long slices

4 or 5 medium plum tomatoes, seeded and chopped

1 green bell pepper, seeded and cut into slices

1 red bell pepper, seeded and cut into slices

6 cups cooked long-grain rice (see sidebar), for serving

When I was a teenager, this was my favorite dish that my mom made. As an adult working long days outside of the home, I figured out how to make it in my slow cooker, and never looked back! It pretty much cooks itself. Serve it over fluffy rice, and you're done!

1   Lightly spray the inside of a 6-quart slow cooker with oil and put the steak in the cooker. Add the Worcestershire sauce, flour, paprika, and seasoning mix and toss to coat. Add the onion, tomatoes, and green and red bell peppers.

2   Cover and cook on low for 8 hours. To serve, spoon the steak, vegetables, and juices over the prepared rice.

lightened up

To make this dish even lighter, serve the steak over cauliflower "rice." Grate a head of cauliflower on the largest holes of a box grater or with a food processor. In a large skillet set over medium heat, heat 1 tablespoon olive oil until it shimmers. Add the cauliflower and cook, stirring, until tender, 10 to 12 minutes. Add ½ teaspoon kosher salt or Stone House Seasoning (page 226). You won't miss the rice!

leftover makeover

CHEESESTEAK SANDWICH

Reheat the pepper steak in a medium skillet set over medium heat. Split a loaf of French bread three-quarters of the way open. Pile the pepper steak on the bread and top with shredded provolone cheese. Tent the sandwiches with foil and let the cheese melt from the heat of the pepper steak. Serve warm.

freezer friendly

Let the cooked pepper steak and rice cool completely. Portion the pepper steak and rice into separate sealable freezer bags, removing as much air as possible. Place both bags in a third larger freezer bag. Freeze for up to 3 months. To reheat, thaw in the refrigerator overnight. Reheat in a 350°F oven until warmed through, 20 to 30 minutes.

SLOW COOKER HONEY-GLAZED HAM

SERVES 8 TO 10

Oil mister or cooking spray

5- to 6-pound fully cooked spiral-sliced bone-in ham

1 cup packed dark brown sugar

½ cup honey

½ cup yellow mustard

¼ cup pineapple juice

In our family, ham is a required dish for Easter, Thanksgiving (in addition to the turkey), and New Year's—not to mention so many of the Sunday suppers in between. One year, to save precious oven space, I decided to pop my ham into the slow cooker. It has done the job ever since!

1 Lightly spray a 6- to 7-quart slow cooker with oil. Put the ham in the cooker.

2 In a medium bowl, combine the brown sugar, honey, yellow mustard, and pineapple juice. Brush the mixture all over the ham.

3 Cover and cook on low for 8 hours.

leftover makeover

SOUTHERN HAM TEA BISCUITS
Make Grandmother Earlene's Biscuits (page 174) and cut them out with a 1½-inch biscuit cutter. Split the cooked biscuits and spread with a honey mustard made of equal parts honey and mustard. Stuff the biscuits with thin slices of the ham. This is a signature Southern treat that we all love as an appetizer!

freezer friendly
Let the cooked ham cool completely, slice, and divide it among sealable freezer bags. Freeze for up to 3 months. To serve, thaw in the refrigerator overnight and then reheat as needed.

CASSEROLES & ONE-DISH SUPPERS

NEVER-FAIL-ME HAM *and* SPINACH QUICHE

SERVES 8

1 tablespoon olive oil

2 cups fresh spinach

½ medium onion, chopped

6 large eggs

1 cup milk

½ teaspoon kosher salt

½ teaspoon freshly ground black pepper

1 cup chopped cooked ham

1½ cups grated Cheddar cheese

1 unbaked Perfect Piecrust (recipe follows)

Quiche isn't just for breakfast or brunch! I love to make this for a simple weeknight supper and serve it with fruit and a green salad. Even though I skip the heavy cream, my version is wonderfully creamy and scrumptious! The best part is how easy it is to whip together. In fact, I generally make two at a time—one to eat now and one to freeze for later. That way, I've solved the dilemma of what's for supper twice!

1 Preheat the oven to 375°F.

2 In a medium skillet set over medium-low heat, heat the olive oil. Add the spinach and onion, and cook, stirring, until just tender, about 3 minutes. Transfer to a plate.

3 In a medium bowl, whisk together the eggs, milk, salt, and pepper until light and foamy. Stir in the cooked spinach and onion along with the ham and cheese. Pour the filling into the pie shell.

4 Bake until the filling is set and the top is lightly browned, 35 to 45 minutes. Remove the dish from the oven and let the quiche rest for 5 minutes before cutting.

lightened up
Skip the piecrust and turn this quiche into a frittata instead! Once you've stirred together the cooked spinach, onion, ham and cheese into the egg mixture, coat an ovenproof skillet with olive oil to prevent sticking. Then, pour the egg mixture into the prepared skillet and bake as directed.

freezer friendly
Let the cooked quiche cool completely. Wrap it tightly in plastic wrap, place in a freezer bag, and freeze for up to 3 months. To reheat, thaw in the refrigerator overnight and then heat in a 325°F oven until warmed through, about 30 minutes.

(recipe continues)

southern hospitality

Preheat the oven to 425° F. Coat a muffin tin with olive oil. Make the Perfect Pie Crust and cut the rolled-out dough into 2½-inch circles with a cookie cutter. Press them into the prepared tin. Fill with the quiche mixture and bake until the filling is set, about 15 minutes.

PERFECT PIECRUST

MAKES ONE 9-INCH PIECRUST

4 tablespoons (½ stick) salted butter, plus more for the dish

1½ cups all-purpose flour, plus more for rolling the dough

½ teaspoon kosher salt

¼ cup shortening

4 to 5 tablespoons ice water

1   Butter a 9-inch pie plate or skillet.

2   In a large bowl, combine the flour and salt. Using a pastry blender or two forks, cut in the shortening and butter until the mixture resembles a coarse meal. While stirring with a wooden spoon, gradually add ice water until a ball of dough forms.

3   Put the dough on a lightly floured piece of plastic wrap and form it into a disc. Lightly flour the top of the pie dough and place another sheet of plastic wrap on top. Working from the center, roll the dough about ⅛ inch thick. Remove the top piece of plastic, fold the dough in half, and lay the dough across the pie plate. Remove the bottom piece of plastic and unfold the dough. Press the dough lightly into the bottom and sides of the pie plate. Wrap well with a piece of the plastic wrap and freeze for at least 30 minutes, or up to overnight.

4   If parbaking (also called blind baking), preheat the oven to 425°F. Using a fork, lightly prick the bottom and sides of the dough. Bake the piecrust until lightly browned, about 8 minutes.

5   If not parbaking, proceed according to the recipe instructions.

SPICY STUFFED CABBAGE ROLLS

SERVES 6

Oil mister or cooking spray

1 cup Sweet and Spicy BBQ
sauce (page 217)

1½ pounds ground beef

1½ cups cooked long-grain
rice (see page 92)

1 small onion, chopped

1 large egg, beaten

1 teaspoon Worcestershire
sauce

2 tablespoons chopped
fresh parsley

1½ teaspoons Stone House
Seasoning (page 226)

½ teaspoon chili powder

1 medium head of cabbage
(about 3 pounds)

freezer friendly
Portion the cooked cabbage
rolls into freezer containers
and freeze for up to
3 months. To serve, thaw in
the refrigerator overnight.
Reheat in a 350°F oven until
warmed through, about
20 minutes.

Stuffed cabbage rolls may sound a bit tedious, but they're actually quite simple. One helpful trick: Cook the cabbage whole, which makes removing the cabbage leaves a cinch. Once stuffed and baked in the Sweet and Spicy BBQ Sauce, they become incredibly tender and taste absolutely amazing!

1   Preheat the oven to 350°F. Lightly spray a 9 × 13-inch baking dish with oil. Spoon ½ cup of the barbecue sauce into the dish and set aside.

2   In a large bowl, using clean hands, mix together the ground beef, rice, onion, egg, Worcestershire sauce, parsley, seasoning mix, and chili powder. Set aside.

3   In a large Dutch oven or stockpot, bring 2 cups water to a boil. Remove the core from the cabbage. Put the cabbage in the pot core side down. Cover and cook over medium heat until the leaves soften, about 15 minutes. Transfer to a colander.

4   Gently remove the leaves from the cabbage, being careful not to tear them. Cut out the hard center vein of the leaves. Spoon ¼ cup of the meat mixture into the center of a cabbage leaf. Roll the leaf around the mixture, tightly tucking in the sides as you roll. Nestle the roll, seam side down, into the sauce in the casserole dish. Repeat until you have 12 rolls. Pour the remaining ½ cup barbecue sauce over the rolls and cover tightly with foil.

5   Bake until the cabbage is tender and the filling is cooked through, 30 to 35 minutes.

even easier!
My unstuffed version of these cabbage rolls is perfect for weeknight cooking. Chop the cabbage and set it aside. In a Dutch oven set over medium heat, cook the ground beef and onion until the meat is browned and the onion is tender, 7 to 10 minutes. Drain off the fat, and then add the Worcestershire sauce, seasoning mix, chili powder, 1 cup water, and the chopped cabbage (skip the egg). Bring to a boil, cover, and reduce the heat to medium. Cook until the cabbage is tender, about 25 minutes. Stir in the cooked rice, BBQ sauce, top with the parsley, and serve.

MUSHROOM *and* WILD RICE– STUFFED PEPPERS

SERVES 6

6 medium red, yellow, or green peppers, halved and seeded

1½ cups tomato sauce, homemade (page 229) or store-bought

1½ cups cooked wild rice

1 cup shredded Parmesan cheese

4 cups chopped baby portobello mushrooms

½ medium onion, chopped

2 garlic cloves, minced

2 teaspoons chopped fresh oregano or 1 teaspoon dried

½ teaspoon kosher salt

I've always been a fan of stuffed peppers. They're filling, look nice on the plate, and have a good dose of veggies in a flavorful little package. The mushrooms in my version provide plenty of meaty deliciousness for a perfect vegetarian meal where no one misses the meat. They're very easy to assemble—especially if you cook the rice a day ahead—and take only thirty minutes to make. You'll have dinner on the table in no time!

1   Preheat the oven to 425°F. Place the pepper halves, cut sides up, in 9 × 13-inch baking dish and set aside.

2   In a medium bowl, combine the tomato sauce, wild rice, ½ cup of the Parmesan cheese, the mushrooms, onion, garlic, oregano, and salt. Divide among the pepper halves and cover tightly with foil.

3   Bake for 20 minutes. Remove the foil and sprinkle the remaining ½ cup Parmesan cheese on top of the peppers and bake until golden, 5 minutes. Serve hot.

leftover makeover

STUFFED PEPPER SOUP
Chop the leftover stuffed peppers into bite-sized pieces and put them in a Dutch oven set over medium heat. Pour in enough tomato sauce (page 229) to cover the peppers and filling by about 2 inches. Bring to a boil, cover, and reduce the heat to low. Simmer until heated through, about 15 minutes. Serve with sprinklings of Stone House Seasoning and Parmesan cheese.

freezer friendly

Let the cooked stuffed peppers cool completely. Portion into freezer containers and freeze for up to 3 months. To serve, thaw in the refrigerator overnight. Tent with foil and reheat in a 350°F oven until warmed through, about 20 minutes.

JAMBALAYA

SERVES 6 TO 8

½ pound andouille or
smoked sausage, sliced

½ medium onion, chopped

½ cup chopped celery

1 large green bell
pepper, chopped

2 garlic cloves, minced

2 teaspoons Blackening
Seasoning (page 226)

1 teaspoon dried thyme

1 teaspoon dried oregano

2 medium plum tomatoes,
chopped

2 cups chicken stock,
homemade (at right)
or store-bought

1 cup uncooked
long-grain rice

1 pound shrimp, peeled
and deveined

½ cup chopped
fresh parsley

Jambalaya is a spicy surf-and-turf meal, and my recipe comes together in a snap! Made with andouille sausage, shrimp, vegetables, and rice, the whole dish cooks in one pan and goes perfectly from stovetop to table in thirty minutes. If you prefer a less spicy meat, use smoked sausage instead of andouille.

1   In a medium saucepan set over high heat, combine the sausage, onion, celery, bell pepper, garlic, blackening seasoning, thyme and oregano. Cook, stirring, until the vegetables are tender, about 3 minutes. Stir in the tomatoes, chicken stock, and rice. Bring to a boil. Cover, reduce the heat to medium, and simmer, stirring occasionally, until the rice is tender, about 15 minutes.

2   Stir in the shrimp, cover, and cook until the shrimp are pink, 3 to 5 minutes. Remove the pan from the heat and stir in the parsley. Serve immediately.

HOW TO
make chicken stock

Simmer a whole chicken, an onion, a garlic clove, 2 celery stalks, 2 carrots, 1 teaspoon kosher salt, 1 teaspoon freshly ground black pepper, 1 bunch of fresh thyme, and about 5 quarts water for about 4 hours. Strain off the stock, discarding the vegetables and saving the chicken for another use. Transfer the stock to freezer-safe containers. Freeze for up to 1 year.

WEEKNIGHT CHICKEN POT PIE

SERVES 6 TO 8

4 skinless, boneless chicken breasts, cut into ½-inch pieces

2 cups peeled and chopped potatoes

2 cups chopped carrots

1 cup sliced celery

2 tablespoons olive oil

½ teaspoon kosher salt

2 cups Cream of Chicken Soup (recipe follows)

2 cups self-rising flour

1 cup buttermilk

6 tablespoons salted butter, melted

Traditional chicken pot pie, with a lovely double crust, can take quite a bit of time to prepare. So I came up with a recipe that's faster and leaves you with just one pot to clean—much easier! I've also found that my pot pie is really versatile. Here, I've used the classic vegetable mix of potatoes, carrots, and celery—which happen to be my favorites—but it's great with other vegetables as well. I also make a version with mushrooms and caramelized onions, and another with parsnips and leeks.

1   Preheat the oven to 475°F.

2   Put the chicken in a 3-quart Dutch oven set over medium heat and cover with water by about 1 inch. Add the potatoes, carrots, celery, olive oil, and salt. Bring to a boil, then reduce the heat, cover, and simmer until the chicken is cooked through and the potatoes are tender, 8 to 10 minutes. Drain the liquid, reserving 1 cup. Stir in the soup.

3   In a medium bowl, combine the flour, buttermilk, and melted butter. Pour over the chicken mixture.

4   Bake until the topping has risen and turned golden brown, 12 to 15 minutes. Let cool for about 5 minutes before serving.

southern hospitality

Assemble pot pies in everything from individual ramekins to family-size casseroles to make a freezer-friendly meal that's perfect for sharing! Just grab a pie from the freezer and take it and a green salad to a family welcoming a new baby or a friend who's under the weather.

freezer friendly

Let the cooked pot pie cool completely, then portion into freezer containers and freeze for up to 3 months. To serve, thaw in the refrigerator overnight. Tent with foil and reheat in a 350°F oven until warmed through, about 20 minutes.

(recipe continues)

make self-rising flour

If you don't have self-rising flour on hand, make your own by whisking together 1 cup all-purpose flour, 1½ teaspoons baking powder, and ¼ teaspoon kosher salt.

CREAM OF CHICKEN SOUP

MAKES 4 CUPS

3 tablespoons salted butter

¼ cup all-purpose flour

3 cups chicken stock, homemade (page 104) or store-bought

1 cup whole milk, half-and-half, or cream

½ teaspoon kosher salt

½ teaspoon freshly ground white or black pepper

¼ teaspoon onion powder (optional)

¼ teaspoon garlic powder (optional)

In a medium saucepan set over low heat, melt the butter. Whisk in 2 tablespoons of the flour and cook, whisking frequently, until it turns a light sandy color, 4 to 5 minutes. Whisk in the remaining 2 tablespoons flour. Slowly, about 1 cup at a time, whisk in the chicken stock and milk. Bring to a simmer and cook until thick and creamy, about 15 minutes. Remove the pan from the heat and stir in the salt and pepper, as well as the onion and garlic powders, if using.

MAMA'S MEAT LOAF *with* SWEET *and* SPICY BBQ SAUCE

SERVES 6

1 cup tomato sauce, homemade (page 229), or store-bought

1 large egg, beaten

1 teaspoon Worcestershire sauce

1 cup dried bread crumbs, homemade (page 63) or store-bought

½ teaspoon kosher salt

1½ pounds ground beef

½ cup finely chopped onion

½ cup Sweet and Spicy BBQ Sauce (page 217)

Mama's meat loaf is legendary in my family, and it was one of the first recipes of hers that I made for Bart when we were dating. I'm not certain, but I think it might be one of the things that encouraged him to pop the question. And now, some twenty years later, it is still one of his favorite meals. It's easy to see why. The meat loaf stays moist and tender, and the barbecue sauce adds a sweet and spicy touch. Thankfully, it couldn't be easier to make!

1 Preheat the oven to 325°F.

2 In a small bowl, combine the tomato sauce, egg, Worcestershire sauce, bread crumbs, and salt.

3 In a large bowl, using clean hands, combine the ground beef and onion. Add the tomato sauce mixture and mix until everything is well blended. Transfer the mixture to a 5½ × 9½-inch loaf pan.

4 Bake until cooked through, 45 minutes to 1 hour. Remove the pan from the oven and pour off any liquid. Reduce the oven temperature to 300°F. Cover the meat loaf with ¼ cup of the barbecue sauce. Bake until the sauce is thick and lightly browned around the edges, about 15 minutes. Serve with the remaining ¼ cup sauce on the side.

even easier!

If you are short on time, make individual servings by scooping the meat loaf mixture into muffin tins that have been lightly sprayed with oil. Bake at 375°F for 20 to 25 minutes, until cooked through. Pour off any liquid, top with barbecue sauce, and bake until the sauce is thick and lightly browned around the edges, about 5 more minutes. Serve with more sauce on the side.

freezer friendly

I love baking the meat loaf in muffin tins (see Even Easier!) so I have individual servings in the freezer. Let the "muffins" cool completely. Pop into the freezer for about 15 minutes. Transfer to sealable freezer bags and freeze for up to 3 months. To serve, thaw in the refrigerator overnight. Tent with foil and reheat in a 350°F oven until warmed through, about 20 minutes. You can also reheat them straight from the freezer in a 350°F oven for about 45 minutes.

CHEESY SPINACH-STUFFED CHICKEN BREASTS

SERVES 6

6 boneless, skinless chicken breasts

½ teaspoon Stone House Seasoning (page 226)

2 tablespoons olive oil

4 cups fresh spinach

½ medium onion, chopped

1 garlic clove, minced

6 ounces mozzarella cheese, shredded

1 (4-ounce) block of Parmesan cheese, grated

When I worked in a corporate job, I'd turn to this recipe if I'd had a particularly bad day. Pounding the chicken helped release all the stress of the office! Then, when Sam was just a little fella, I enjoyed making it with him because he would climb up on his little stool beside the kitchen counter and "help" me pound that chicken flat as could be with our rolling pins. Maybe he had a few stresses he needed to get rid of too. And now, I love making it just for reliving the memory of how he'd say, "I think we got it, Mama."

1　Preheat the oven to 350°F. Line a rimmed baking sheet with parchment paper.

2　Put the chicken breasts in a large sealable bag and, using a mallet or rolling pin, carefully pound until ½ inch thick. Transfer the chicken to the prepared baking sheet and sprinkle with the seasoning mix.

3　In medium ovenproof skillet set over medium heat, heat 1 tablespoon of the olive oil. Add the spinach, onion, and garlic, and cook, stirring, until the spinach has wilted and the onion is tender, about 3 minutes. Spread a layer of the spinach mixture over each piece of chicken. Top with both cheeses. Roll each piece of chicken tightly around the spinach and cheeses. Secure with toothpicks, if needed.

4　In the same skillet, heat the remaining 1 tablespoon olive oil over medium heat until it begins to shimmer. Place the rolled chicken, seam side down, in the skillet and cook until lightly browned on all sides, 2 to 3 minutes per side. Transfer the skillet to the oven.

5　Bake until the chicken is cooked through and a thermometer inserted in the thickest part registers 165°F, 15 to 20 minutes. Let rest for about 5 minutes before serving.

freezer friendly

Let the cooked stuffed chicken cool completely. Transfer to freezer containers and freeze for up to 3 months. To serve, thaw in the refrigerator overnight. Tent with foil and reheat in a 350°F oven until warmed through, about 20 minutes.

leftover makeover

SPINACH-STUFFED CHICKEN PASTA SALAD

Cook rotini noodles according to the package instructions. Drain. Combine 1 cup sliced kalamata olives, 1 pint halved grape tomatoes, 2 tablespoons diced red onion, and 1 medium peeled, diced cucumber. Toss with the pasta. In a Mason jar, combine ¼ cup olive oil, 2 tablespoons red wine vinegar, ½ teaspoon Dijon mustard, and ½ teaspoon Stone House Seasoning and shake well. Slice the leftover chicken, place it over the pasta salad, and drizzle with the dressing.

BAKED CHICKEN SPAGHETTI

SERVES 6

Oil mister or cooking spray

2 tablespoons olive oil

4 skinless, boneless chicken breasts, cut into 2-inch pieces

1 medium sweet onion, chopped

1 teaspoon kosher salt

1 pound spaghetti, broken into 4-inch pieces

3 cups Cream of Chicken Soup (page 108)

1 cup shredded mozzarella cheese

½ cup shredded Parmesan cheese

Most everybody in the South has a recipe for chicken spaghetti, since it's usually a crowd pleaser. I like to cook the pasta in the same Dutch oven used for browning the chicken; you get more of the flavor of the chicken that way. I've also updated the classic with homemade cream of chicken soup, which tastes much fresher than the canned version.

1   Preheat the oven to 350°F. Lightly spray a 2-quart baking dish with oil.

2   In a Dutch oven set over medium heat, heat the olive oil. Add the chicken and cook until browned, 8 to 10 minutes. Add the onion and cook, stirring, until softened, about 5 more minutes. Transfer to a large bowl.

3   Add 4 quarts water and the salt to the Dutch oven and bring to a boil over medium-high heat. Add the spaghetti and cook until al dente, 5 to 6 minutes. Transfer to a colander to drain. Return the noodles to the warm pot and stir in the chicken mixture and soup. Pour the mixture into the prepared baking dish and top with the mozzarella and Parmesan cheeses.

4   Bake until the cheese is golden brown, about 15 minutes.

lightened up
Use zucchini ribbons in place of spaghetti to not only lighten the recipe, but reduce the total cooking time!

freezer friendly
Portion the cooked chicken spaghetti into freezer containers and freeze for up to 3 months. To serve, thaw in the refrigerator overnight. Tent with foil and reheat in a 350°F oven until warmed through, about 20 minutes.

SAUSAGE *and* GRITS CASSEROLE

SERVES 8

Oil mister or cooking spray

1 pound mild breakfast sausage, crumbled

½ medium onion, chopped

1 medium jalapeño pepper, seeded and chopped

1 garlic clove, minced

2 cups milk

½ cup quick-cooking grits

4 large eggs, beaten

½ teaspoon dry mustard

½ teaspoon dried thyme

½ teaspoon freshly ground black pepper

1 cup grated Cheddar cheese

freezer friendly

Let the cooked casserole cool completely. Transfer to freezer containers and freeze for up to 3 months. To serve, thaw in the refrigerator overnight. Tent with foil and reheat in a 325°F oven until warmed through, 30 minutes.

While many might consider this a breakfast casserole, my family loves it for supper. This actually came about by accident. One night I pulled a casserole from my freezer to thaw overnight for the next night's supper, but didn't pay much attention to what I was doing. When I was ready to put it in the oven, I realized I had grabbed the sausage and grits casserole I had prepared for Christmas brunch! Without anything else planned for our meal besides a salad, I went with it, and we've been enjoying it as a supper ever since. Sometimes, accidents lead to the best discoveries!

1 Preheat the oven to 350°F. Lightly spray a 9 × 13-inch casserole dish with oil.

2 In a medium skillet set over medium heat, cook the sausage, using a wooden spoon to break it up as it cooks, about 3 minutes. Add the onion, jalapeño, and garlic and cook until the onion is soft and translucent and the sausage has browned, 3 to 5 minutes more. Using a slotted spoon, transfer the mixture to a large bowl and let cool while you prepare the grits.

3 In a 3-quart saucepan set over medium-low heat, bring 2 cups water and the milk to a low boil. Whisking constantly, gradually pour in the grits. Cook, whisking constantly so that lumps do not form, until thick and creamy, 3 to 5 minutes. Pour the grits into the bowl with the sausage mixture and stir until well-combined. Stir in the eggs, mustard, thyme, and pepper. Pour into the prepared casserole dish.

4 Bake until lightly browned and completely set when shaken lightly, about 30 minutes.

5 Remove from the oven and top with the cheese. Bake until the cheese has melted, 5 more minutes.

southern hospitality

Take this casserole, along with my Poppy Seed Fruit Salad (page 164), as a hostess gift for your host's breakfast the next morning. She'll be forever grateful not to have to cook the morning after a dinner party!

WHITE CHICKEN ENCHILADA STUFFED SHELLS

SERVES 6

12 large pasta shells

3 or 4 cooked chicken breasts, shredded

1½ cups shredded Monterey Jack cheese

2 tablespoons salted butter

2 tablespoons all-purpose flour

2 cups chicken stock, homemade (page 104) or store-bought

1 cup Greek yogurt or sour cream

1 medium jalapeño, seeded and chopped

½ teaspoon ground cumin

½ teaspoon Stone House Seasoning (page 226)

Stuffing pasta shells with an enchilada-style filling might not sound like the most logical choice, but I think you'll love these! Made with tender chicken and my white enchilada sauce, this casserole is ready and on the table in thirty minutes. If you like your enchiladas with a bit more kick, add more jalapeños.

1   Preheat the oven to 350°F.

2   Bring a large pot of water to a boil. Add the pasta shells and cook until just softened, about 10 minutes. Using a slotted spoon, transfer the shells to a colander.

3   Meanwhile, in a large bowl, combine the shredded chicken and 1¼ cups of the cheese. Spoon the mixture into the shells and arrange the stuffed shells in a 9 × 13-inch baking dish.

4   In a medium saucepan set over medium heat, melt the butter. Whisk in the flour and cook, whisking constantly, until lightly browned, about 1 minute. Add the chicken stock and cook, whisking, until thick and bubbly, about 3 more minutes. Remove the pan from the heat and stir in the yogurt, jalapeño, cumin, and seasoning mix. Pour the sauce over the stuffed shells and top with the remaining ¼ cup cheese.

5   Bake until the shells are warmed through and the cheese is melted, about 15 minutes.

freezer friendly

Let the cooked shells cool completely. Portion them into freezer containers and freeze for up to 3 months. To serve, thaw in the refrigerator overnight. Reheat in a 325°F oven until warmed through, 30 minutes.

WEEKNIGHT BEEF *and* BEAN CASSEROLE *with* CORNBREAD TOPPING

SERVES 6 TO 8

1 pound ground beef

½ medium onion, chopped

1 garlic clove, minced

1 jalapeño, seeded and chopped

2 cups dried pinto beans, cooked (see sidebar)

2 cups tomato sauce, homemade (page 229) or store-bought

1 medium tomato, chopped

1 cup grated Cheddar cheese

1 cup self-rising yellow cornmeal mix

½ cup self-rising flour

1 large egg

1 cup buttermilk

Winters in the South are known to be sunny and mild, but every once in a while, we are faced with snow and ice. That's when you'd think the end of the world was upon us! A few years back, we had an ice storm that knocked out power for days. I pulled out my daddy's cast-iron Dutch oven and made this casserole on a bed of coals in the fireplace. It worked like a charm and made us feel like we'd get through the storm after all!

1   Preheat the oven to 400°F.

2   In a large ovenproof skillet or Dutch oven set over medium heat, cook the ground beef, breaking up the meat with a wooden spoon, until browned through, 3 to 5 minutes. Drain the fat from the meat. Add the onion, garlic, jalapeño, pinto beans, tomato sauce, and tomato and remove the pan from the heat. Top with the cheese.

3   In a medium bowl, combine the cornmeal, flour, egg, and buttermilk. Pour the mixture on top of the meat mixture.

4   Bake until the cornbread topping is lightly browned, 15 to 20 minutes. Serve hot.

freezer friendly

Let the cooked dish cool completely. Transfer to a freezer container and freeze for up to 3 months. To serve, thaw in the refrigerator overnight. Reheat in a 325°F oven until warmed through, about 20 minutes.

BROWN SUGAR BAKED SALMON *and* VEGETABLES

SERVES 6

1 whole salmon fillet (about 2 pounds)

3 medium squash, thinly sliced

2 medium zucchini, thinly sliced

1 medium onion, thinly sliced

2 tablespoons olive oil

1 teaspoon kosher salt

½ teaspoon freshly ground black pepper

¼ cup packed dark brown sugar

1½ teaspoons stone-ground mustard

Salmon is another favorite fish in my house. I could eat it every single day and be a happy girl! And it's so good for you too. This savory-sweet one-dish meal is one of my favorite ways to prepare it—especially for busy weeknights. I prefer to use wild-caught Alaskan salmon, so I stock up when it's in season or I find a great sale.

1   Preheat the oven to 425°F. Line a rimmed baking sheet with parchment paper or foil.

2   Place the salmon, skin side down, on the prepared baking sheet. Arrange the vegetables alongside the salmon around the edges of the baking sheet. Drizzle the vegetables with the olive oil. Sprinkle the salmon and vegetables with the salt and pepper. Cover the fish and vegetables with another piece of parchment paper or foil. Bake for 10 minutes.

3   Meanwhile, in a small bowl, combine the brown sugar and mustard.

4   Remove the salmon and vegetables from the oven and remove the top piece of parchment paper or foil. Spread the brown sugar mixture over the salmon and return the pan to the oven. Bake until the salmon is firm to the touch and a thermometer inserted in the thickest part registers 135°F, about 15 minutes.

leftover makeover

SALMON WITH SPINACH AND EGG
Sauté fresh spinach in a bit of olive oil until wilted. Transfer to a plate and top with some leftover salmon, veggies, and a poached or fried egg.

CHICKEN *and* SNAP PEA SKEWERS

SERVES 4 TO 6

3 boneless, skinless chicken breasts, cut into 2-inch pieces

½ cup Mint and Parsley Pesto (recipe follows)

Oil mister or cooking spray

48 sugar snap peas

1 medium red onion, cut into 8 wedges

I love making these skewers as soon as my snap peas are at their peak. They're quick to assemble and pretty enough to serve when company comes. Marinating the chicken in the mint and parsley pesto ensures it is as juicy as it is flavorful. I love to prep them the night before so they marinate overnight in the refrigerator which makes the meal even easier when it's time to cook. Once broiled, the snap peas are tender and the onion is caramelized and sweetened to perfection.

1   Put the chicken in a large sealable bag or glass bowl. Add ¼ cup of the pesto and toss to coat well. Remove as much air as possible from the bag, seal (or cover the bowl with wrap), and refrigerate for at least 1 hour or up to overnight.

2   Put an oven rack in the second-highest position and preheat the broiler. Line a rimmed baking sheet with foil and lightly spray with oil.

3   Thread the chicken, snap peas, and onion layers onto 8-inch skewers, alternating as you go. Place the skewers onto the prepared baking sheet.

4   Broil, turning halfway through, until the chicken has cooked through, about 10 minutes. Let rest for about 3 minutes; then serve with the remaining ¼ cup pesto drizzled over the top.

(recipe continues)

MINT AND PARSLEY PESTO

MAKES ½ CUP

1 medium garlic clove

¼ cup raw walnuts

1 cup fresh mint, packed

1½ cups packed fresh parsley

½ teaspoon kosher salt

½ teaspoon freshly ground black pepper

½ cup olive oil

½ cup freshly grated Parmesan cheese

1 Place the garlic and walnuts in a food processor fitted with the chopping blade or in a high-speed blender. Process until the garlic and walnuts are in fine pieces, about 20 seconds. Add the mint, parsley, salt, and pepper. With the processor running, slowly pour the olive oil through the feed tube. Process until the pesto is completely pureed and smooth, scraping down the sides as needed, about 1 minute. Add the Parmesan and process for 1 minute to incorporate.

2 Use immediately or refrigerate in an airtight container for up to 3 days. The color of the pesto will darken slightly in the refrigerator, but it will still taste delicious.

ONE-PAN ROASTED PORK CHOPS *with* VEGETABLES

SERVES 6

2 tablespoons olive oil

6 (8-ounce) bone-in pork chops

1 bunch of asparagus, tough ends trimmed

12 ounces fresh or frozen and thawed Brussels sprouts, trimmed and halved

4 carrots, cut into 2-inch pieces

1½ teaspoons Stone House Seasoning (page 226)

It can't get any easier than tossing an entire meal onto a baking sheet and cooking the whole thing in the oven. That's what we have here, and boy, is it a hit in my family. The bone gives the lean pork meat a deeper, richer flavor and the vegetables become tender and delicious, with no need for any heavy sauces.

1 Preheat the oven to 400°F. Grease a rimmed baking sheet with 1 tablespoon of the olive oil.

2 Arrange the pork chops, asparagus, Brussels sprouts, and carrots on the prepared baking sheet. Drizzle with the remaining 1 tablespoon olive oil and toss well. Sprinkle with the Stone House Seasoning.

3 Bake until the pork chops are cooked through and a thermometer inserted in the thickest part registers 145°F, about 20 minutes. Set the oven on broil and cook until the vegetables are caramelized further, 3 minutes. Serve immediately.

freezer friendly

Let the cooked dish cool completely. Transfer to sealable freezer bags and freeze for up to 3 months. To serve, let thaw in the refrigerator overnight. Then reheat in a 325°F oven on a rimmed baking sheet tented with foil until warmed through, about 20 minutes.

ONE-PAN PARMESAN-CRUSTED CHICKEN *with* BROCCOLI

SERVES 6

2 tablespoons olive oil

6 (7-ounce) boneless, skinless chicken breasts

12 ounces fresh or frozen broccoli florets

1 teaspoon Stone House Seasoning (page 226)

2 garlic cloves, minced

½ cup freshly grated Parmesan cheese

¼ cup chopped fresh parsley

freezer friendly

Let the cooked dish cool completely. Portion it into freezer containers and freeze for up to 3 months. To serve, thaw in the refrigerator overnight. Reheat in a 325°F oven until warmed through 20 minutes.

Like every other family I know, our afternoons are filled with activities—homework, Scouts, youth group, and the like. It seems like every day there is something on the schedule that requires us to be away from home into the evening. Those nights, I count on recipes like this one, where I can toss everything onto a baking sheet, throw it in the oven, and be at the table eating in no time.

1 Preheat the oven to 425°F. Grease a rimmed baking sheet with 1 tablespoon of the olive oil.

2 Arrange the chicken breasts in the center of the prepared baking sheet. Arrange the broccoli around the chicken. Drizzle the broccoli with the remaining 1 tablespoon olive oil and sprinkle everything with the Stone House seasoning.

3 Bake until the chicken breasts are cooked through and a thermometer inserted in the thickest part registers 160°F, 25 to 30 minutes.

4 In a small bowl, combine the garlic, Parmesan, and parsley. Top each chicken breast with some of the mixture. Broil until the cheese is melted and the broccoli is deeply browned, 3 minutes. Remove the pan from the oven, tent with foil, and let rest for 5 minutes. Serve warm.

leftover makeover

PARMESAN CHICKEN AND BROCCOLI MAC AND CHEESE
Chop 3 chicken breasts leftover from Parmesan chicken and broccoli into 1½-inch pieces. Cook 2 cups elbow noodles according to package directions and drain. Meanwhile, melt 2 tablespoons salted butter in a large skillet set over medium heat. Whisk in 2 tablespoons all-purpose flour and cook, whisking, until lightly browned, about 3 minutes. Whisk in 1¼ cups half-and-half. Stir in 1 cup each of shredded Cheddar and Monterey Jack cheese until melted, 3 to 5 minutes. Stir in the chopped leftovers and the noodles. Cook for 5 more minutes, until warmed through, and serve.

SIMPLE SIDES

GREEN BEANS *with* NEW POTATOES

SERVES 6 TO 8

1 tablespoon olive oil

1 medium onion, chopped

2 pounds fresh or frozen and thawed green beans, trimmed

10 small new potatoes

1 garlic clove, minced

1 cup chicken stock, homemade (page 104) or store-bought

2 teaspoons apple cider vinegar

½ teaspoon kosher salt

Green beans fresh from the garden are delicious any way that you cook them. But I think they definitely shine in this family favorite, alongside small new potatoes and with a tangy hint of apple cider vinegar. To make quick work of trimming fresh green beans, I line them up on my cutting board and cut a large bunch at once.

1   In a Dutch oven or large saucepan set over medium heat, heat the oil. Add the onion and cook, stirring, until tender, about 3 minutes. Add the green beans, potatoes, garlic, and chicken stock. Cover and cook until the potatoes and beans are tender, but not mushy, 15 minutes.

2   Transfer to a serving dish. Sprinkle with apple cider vinegar and salt, and serve.

HOW TO
freeze fresh green beans

Freezing fresh beans is simple and a great way to enjoy vegetables from the garden throughout the winter. Trim the ends and remove any strings from the green beans. Bring 1 gallon of water per pound of string beans to boil in a Dutch oven. Carefully drop green beans into boiling water for 3 minutes. Remove with a slotted spoon and plunge into a bowl of ice water. Transfer to a paper towel–lined rimmed baking sheet to dry. Portion into freezer bags, removing as much air as possible as you seal, and freeze for up to 7 months.

BUTTERED CARROTS *with* PEAS *and* THYME

SERVES 6

2 tablespoons salted butter

6 large carrots, cut into ¼-inch slices

1 cup fresh peas or 1 (8-ounce) package frozen peas

1½ teaspoons fresh thyme or ½ teaspoon dried

½ teaspoon kosher salt

¼ teaspoon freshly ground black pepper

I can think of few things that go together as well as peas and carrots. Goodness, we even use them as a comparison to say that other things go well together! However, I'd like to go on record saying that I think butter and thyme round out the flavor even better in this updated classic. And it takes only a little to bring out the buttery flavor of the tender carrots. When I can find carrots in a rainbow of colors, I like to pick a mixture, but you can use all orange ones too. I love to serve this with Sunday Roasted Chicken (page 50).

1 In a large saucepan set over medium heat, melt the butter. Add the carrots and cook, stirring, until fork-tender, 7 to 9 minutes.

2 Stir in the peas, thyme, salt, and pepper and cook, stirring, until the peas are warmed through, 2 to 3 minutes (frozen peas may take a couple of extra minutes).

GRAND-MOTHER EARLENE'S CREAMED CORN

SERVES 6 TO 8

6 ears fresh corn

½ cup whole milk

2 tablespoons salted butter

1 teaspoon kosher salt

Of all the dishes that my Grandmother Earlene made for us, one of my favorites was her creamed corn. I've changed her recipe ever so slightly to lighten it up. I reduced the amount of butter, but kept the creaminess by pureeing the corn, which both thickens the dish and makes it even creamier. I think she would have loved it!

1 Cut the corn kernels from the cobs and put in a Dutch oven or large saucepan (you'll have about 4 cups of kernels). Using the back of a knife, scrape the milk of the corncobs into the pot. Add ¼ cup water and cook, stirring occasionally, over medium heat until the corn is just tender, about 20 minutes.

2 Put about 1 cup of the cooked corn in a blender and pulse until smooth (alternatively, you can use an immersion blender to partially blend the corn). Return it to the pot. Stir in the milk and butter and cook, stirring occasionally, until thickened, 5 minutes. Stir in the salt and serve hot.

freezer friendly

Let the cooked creamed corn cool completely. Transfer to sealable freezer bags and freeze for up to 3 months. To serve, thaw in the refrigerator overnight. Reheat in a medium saucepan over medium heat until warmed through, 15 minutes. If the corn is too thick, add a tablespoon or so of water.

SOUTHERN BUTTER BEANS

SERVES 6

1 pound fresh or frozen and thawed butter beans

3 cups chicken stock, homemade (page 104) or store-bought, or water

1 medium onion, chopped

3 tablespoons olive oil

2 teaspoons Stone House Seasoning (page 226)

½ teaspoon ground cumin

⅛ teaspoon red pepper flakes

There's no better signal than the arrival of butter beans to let us know that spring is here. A member of the lima bean family, they are slightly smaller and have a subtle taste. Afternoons spent on the porch shelling butter beans have never been my favorite pastime, but I'm always thankful after the first bite. I like to use spices for flavor, which lets me reduce the oil considerably. If you want to make this with dried beans instead of fresh, see page 38.

1   In a large pot set over medium-high heat, combine the butter beans, chicken stock, onion, olive oil, seasoning mix, cumin, and red pepper flakes. Bring to a boil and cook for 5 minutes. Skim away and discard any foam that may rise to the top.

2   Cover, reduce the heat to low, and simmer until the beans are tender (they should feel soft when pressed against the side of the pot with the back of a wooden spoon), 30 to 45 minutes. Serve warm.

ROASTED OKRA

SERVES 6 TO 8

1½ pounds fresh or frozen
and thawed okra

1 tablespoon olive oil

1½ teaspoons Stone House
Seasoning (page 226)

I grew up hating okra. Absolutely hating it. One of my chores when I was younger was helping in the garden during the summer and after school. I'd always been told when picking okra to make sure I had on long pants and sleeves. Usually I did, but one day I procrastinated until right before suppertime and ran outside to pick the okra in my shorts and T-shirt. If you've ever picked okra, you know what happened—I was stinging and itching before making it back to the house. I learned my lesson! Nowadays, I love okra. This quick roasted version is much easier and lighter than fried okra, and you still get a nice crunch.

1 Preheat the oven to 450°F.

2 Place the okra on a rimmed baking sheet. Drizzle with the olive oil and sprinkle with the seasoning mix. Toss to coat, and then arrange the okra in a single layer.

3 Roast until tender and golden brown, 12 to 15 minutes.

ROSEMARY ROASTED BEETS, CARROTS, *and* ONIONS

SERVES 6 TO 8

Oil mister or cooking spray

3 medium beets, peeled and halved

3 medium carrots, halved lengthwise

2 medium onions, quartered

3 tablespoons olive oil

2 tablespoons roughly chopped fresh rosemary

1 teaspoon Stone House Seasoning (page 226)

How do I get my son to beg for beets? I roast them with rosemary, carrots, and onions! Roasting transforms them from crunchy and earthy to sweet, caramelized, and tender. This dish is delicious with everything from chicken to pork, and you should definitely try it with Sam's Oven-Fried Halibut (page 63).

1   Preheat the oven to 450°F. Lightly spray a rimmed baking sheet with oil.

2   Arrange the beets, carrots, and onion in a single layer on the prepared baking sheet. Drizzle with olive oil and sprinkle with the rosemary and seasoning mix.

3   Bake until the vegetables are fork-tender, 30 minutes. Let cool for about 3 minutes before serving.

NOT YOUR MOTHER'S BROCCOLI CHEESE CASSEROLE

SERVES 12

Oil mister or cooking spray

3 heads broccoli, cut into florets (about 8 cups)

8 tablespoons (1 stick) salted butter

½ cup all-purpose flour

2 cups whole milk or heavy cream

1 cup grated Monterey Jack cheese

½ teaspoon kosher salt

½ teaspoon freshly ground black or white pepper

⅛ teaspoon cayenne pepper

1 cup sour cream

1 cup grated Cheddar cheese

3 tablespoons dried bread crumbs, homemade (page 63) or store-bought

The broccoli and cheese casserole I grew up eating was made with the then-popular cream soup from a can. When I started making this recipe on my own, I decided it was time to update it. On occasion, I also love to add precooked chicken, like from my Sunday Roasted Chicken (page 50), to make it an even heartier, protein-packed entrée.

1   Preheat the oven to 350°F. Lightly spray a 9 × 13-inch baking dish with oil.

2   Bring a large stockpot of water to a boil and cook the broccoli until just crisp-tender, 3 to 5 minutes. Drain well and transfer to the prepared baking dish.

3   In a small saucepan set over medium heat, melt the butter. Whisk in the flour until well combined, and then whisk in the milk, Monterey Jack cheese, salt, pepper, and cayenne. Reduce the heat to low and cook, whisking constantly, until the sauce has thickened slightly, about 3 minutes. Whisk in the sour cream. Pour the cream sauce over the broccoli. Top with the Cheddar cheese and bread crumbs.

4   Bake until bubbling and lightly browned, 35 to 40 minutes.

freezer friendly

Store the uncooked casserole in a freezer container, wrapped well, for up to 3 months. To serve, thaw in the refrigerator overnight and bake as directed.

CREAMED COLLARD GREENS

SERVES 6

1 tablespoon olive oil

1 pound fresh collard greens, trimmed and chopped

½ medium onion, chopped

1 garlic clove, minced

2 tablespoons salted butter

2 tablespoons all-purpose flour

1 cup whole milk

½ teaspoon Stone House Seasoning (page 226)

Pinch of cayenne pepper

Think of this dish as creamed spinach's country cousin. Rich and delicious, it goes perfectly with beef, chicken, fish, and pork—just like its uptown relative. I've reduced the amount of oil and butter traditionally used and replaced the heavy cream with milk. If collard greens aren't available, use kale, mustard greens, or yes, even turnip greens!

1   In a Dutch oven set over medium heat, heat the oil. Add the collard greens, onion, and garlic and cook, stirring, until the greens are wilted and the onion is tender, about 5 minutes. Reduce the heat to medium-low. Add ¼ cup water, cover, and cook until the collards are tender and all of the water has evaporated, 12 to 15 minutes.

2   Meanwhile, in a small saucepan set over medium heat, melt the butter. Whisk in the flour and cook, whisking constantly, until lightly browned, about 3 minutes. Slowly whisk in the milk and cook, whisking constantly, until thickened, about 3 more minutes. Whisk in the seasoning mix and cayenne. Pour the sauce into the collard greens and cook, stirring often, until thickened, about 5 minutes. Serve warm.

freezer friendly

Store the creamed collard greens in a freezer container, wrapped well, for up to 1 year. To serve, thaw in the refrigerator overnight and reheat in a medium saucepan over medium heat until warmed throughout, about 20 minutes.

BUTTERMILK MASHED POTATOES

SERVES 6 TO 8

3 pounds (6 to 8 medium) russet or Yukon gold potatoes, peeled and cut into 2-inch cubes

1¼ cups buttermilk, at room temperature

4 tablespoons (½ stick) salted butter

1 teaspoon kosher salt

¼ teaspoon freshly ground black pepper (optional)

One thing I've discovered about inviting guests to your home for a meal—they always feel most welcome when you serve comforting, homemade dishes rather than fancy fare. (Well, at least they do at my house.) And in my book nothing fits the bill like mashed potatoes. The buttermilk in this version makes them taste indulgent and decadent, even with less butter!

1 Put the cubed potatoes in a large stockpot or Dutch oven. Add enough water to cover by about 2 inches. Cook over medium heat until the potatoes fall apart when pressed with the back of a spoon or pierced with a fork, about 15 minutes.

2 Drain the potatoes and return them to the pot. Using a potato masher, mash the potatoes until smooth. Slowly stir in the buttermilk. Stir in the butter, salt, and pepper, if using, and serve.

leftover makeover

BUTTERMILK POTATO PANCAKES

Combine about 2 cups leftover buttermilk mashed potatoes, 1 large egg, and ¼ cup all-purpose flour. Drizzle a little canola oil in a medium skillet over medium heat. Using a ¼-cup measure, scoop the batter into the oil and cook until browned, 3 to 5 minutes per side.

SAUTÉED SQUASH, ZUCCHINI, *and* OKRA

SERVES 6 TO 8

1 tablespoon olive oil

3 medium yellow squash, cut into ½-inch slices

3 medium zucchini, cut into ½-inch slices

½ pound fresh okra, cut into ½-inch slices

½ medium onion, chopped

1 teaspoon Stone House Seasoning (page 226)

The most plentiful veggies in my garden are always squash, zucchini, and okra. But I forget this little fact every year when planning my garden and never remember to scale back how much I plant! Out of the abundance, I came up with this quick side dish, which has become a definite favorite of ours. Maybe overplanting is a good thing after all.

1   In a 12-inch skillet set over medium heat, heat the olive oil. Add the squash, zucchini, okra, and onion and cook, stirring, until tender, 8 to 10 minutes.

2   Stir in the seasoning mix and serve.

leftover makeover

VEGGIE QUINOA BOWL

Top cooked quinoa with leftover sautéed squash, zucchini, and okra. Drizzle with a little olive oil, and you have a delicious meal in minutes!

ROASTED MUSHROOMS

SERVES 6 TO 8

2 pounds whole mushrooms

1 tablespoon olive oil

2 garlic cloves, minced

1 teaspoon kosher salt

½ teaspoon freshly ground black pepper

1 tablespoon chopped fresh parsley

I absolutely adore mushrooms. I can't really think of a way that I don't enjoy them, but roasting is my absolute favorite! These mushrooms are ready in a jiffy, go well with everything, and are delicious. They're great served with Coffee-Encrusted Prime Rib (page 55) for a holiday meal, or Balsamic Beef (page 90) for a weeknight.

1   Preheat the oven to 450°F.

2   Clean the mushrooms using a damp paper towel and place on a rimmed baking sheet. Toss with the olive oil, garlic, salt, and pepper.

3   Roast until the mushrooms are tender and juices just begin to pool, about 25 minutes. Sprinkle with the fresh parsley and serve.

leftover makeover

CREAMY MUSHROOM PASTA

Cook fettuccine or spaghetti until al dente according to the package directions. Meanwhile, heat 1 tablespoon olive oil in a medium skillet set over medium heat. Add 1 cup chicken stock and 1 cup cream. Bring to a simmer and cook, whisking constantly, until thickened, about 5 minutes. Add about 1 cup of leftover mushrooms and Stone House Seasoning (page 226) to taste. Serve over the cooked pasta with grated Parmesan cheese and chopped fresh parsley.

FIELD PEAS *and* SNAPS

SERVES 6 TO 8

1 pound fresh or
frozen field peas

1 pound fresh green beans,
trimmed and snapped
in half

2 slices of bacon, chopped

1 medium onion, sliced

2 teaspoons Stone House
Seasoning (page 226)

When I was a little girl, Daddy saved peas from our garden as seed peas for the next year. I'd long forgotten about them until after he passed away. One day, my Uncle James surprised me with a bag of Daddy's field peas, which were perfect to plant in my own garden. They are one of my greatest treasures. In this update to a family favorite, I cut the amount of oil and added seasonings that highlight the fresh peas and green beans.

1   Put the field peas, green beans, bacon, and onion in a large Dutch oven set over high heat and cover them by about 1 inch of water. Bring to a boil, cover, and then reduce to a simmer over medium heat. Cook until the peas are tender (they should feel soft when pressed against the side of the pot with the back of a wooden spoon), about 40 minutes. The peas may produce a bit of foam as they cook; use a spoon to skim the foam from the top of the peas and discard it.

2   Add the seasoning mix and serve.

freezer friendly

Let the cooked dish cool completely. Transfer to freezer bags, removing as much air as possible as you seal. Freeze for up to 3 months. To serve, thaw overnight in the refrigerator. Reheat in a saucepan over medium heat until warmed through, 15 minutes. If the beans are too thick, add a few tablespoons of water or chicken stock.

SOUPS, STEWS, SALADS & SLAW

SAM'S EASY WEEKNIGHT BEEF STEW

SERVES 6 TO 8

1 tablespoon olive oil

3- to 4-pound chuck roast,
cut into 2-inch cubes

1 tablespoon
Worcestershire sauce

2 teaspoons Stone House
Seasoning (page 226)

1 medium onion, cut into
2-inch pieces

2 pounds red potatoes,
cut into 2-inch cubes

3 carrots, cut into
1-inch chunks

3 celery stalks, cut into
1-inch chunks

1 cup tomato sauce,
homemade (page 229) or
store-bought

3 cups beef stock

My son, Sam, absolutely loves beef stew. He requested it one evening for supper when he wasn't feeling well. Normally, this dish cooks for hours on the stovetop, but, determined to have it ready fast to calm his craving, I figured out a way to pack in plenty of flavor in a short amount of time. By quickly browning the roast before adding the seasonings and liquids, you still get the deep flavor you expect without the wait.

1   In a Dutch oven or heavy stockpot set over medium heat, heat the oil. Add the beef and brown on all sides, about 8 minutes. Add the Worcestershire sauce, seasoning mix, onion, potatoes, carrots, and celery and cook, stirring, until the onion is tender, about 3 minutes.

2   Stir in the tomato sauce and beef stock, reduce the heat to low, cover, and cook until the beef and vegetables are tender, about 30 minutes. Serve hot.

leftover makeover

BEEF HASH

Heat about 1 tablespoon olive oil in a medium skillet over medium heat. Add about 2 cups of the meat and vegetables from the stew along with about ¼ cup of the liquid. Cook, breaking up the meat with a wooden spoon as you cook, until heated thoroughly and the liquid has thickened, about 15 minutes.

freezer friendly

Let the cooked stew cool completely. Pour it into freezer bags, removing as much air as possible as you seal, and freeze for up to 3 months. To serve, thaw in the refrigerator overnight. Pour into a saucepan set over medium heat. Cook until warmed through, 15 to 20 minutes. If the stew is too thick, add a little water.

MUSHROOM *and* THYME SOUP

SERVES 6

3 tablespoons salted butter

4 ounces fresh mushrooms, sliced

4 ounces fresh mushrooms, roughly chopped

¼ cup finely chopped onion

3 cups chicken stock, homemade (page 104) or store-bought

¼ cup all-purpose flour

1 cup whole milk or half-and-half

½ teaspoon Stone House Seasoning (page 226)

Fresh thyme leaves, for garnish

Cozy, comforting, and delicious, this soup is one I make time and again throughout the fall and winter. It even makes a beautiful starter for a dinner party or holiday meal. But by cooking it a little longer—about 15 more minutes—you can easily use it in recipes that call for condensed cream of mushroom soup! Use your favorite type of mushroom, or even a mix of varieties for lots of flavor and texture.

1 In a medium saucepan set over low heat, melt 1 tablespoon of the butter. Add both the sliced and the chopped mushrooms along with the onion and cook, stirring, until the onion is tender, about 3 minutes. Add 1 cup of the chicken stock and simmer until the mushrooms are tender, about 10 minutes.

2 Meanwhile, in a large saucepan set over medium heat, melt the remaining 2 tablespoons butter. Add 2 tablespoons of the flour and cook, whisking constantly, until the mixture turns a light sandy color, about 5 minutes. Add the remaining flour and whisk until smooth. Add the remaining 2 cups chicken stock and the milk, about 1 cup at a time, whisking constantly until smooth. Bring to a simmer and cook until the mixture starts to thicken, about 10 minutes. Add the mushroom and onion mixture to the soup and cook until thick and creamy, about 10 minutes. Remove the pan from the heat and stir in the seasoning mix. Garnish with the fresh thyme and serve.

freezer friendly

Let the cooked soup cool completely. Pour it into freezer bags and freeze for up to 3 months. To serve, thaw in the refrigerator overnight. Pour the soup into a medium saucepan set over medium heat. Reheat until warmed through, 10 to 15 minutes.

SLOW COOKER CHICKEN NOODLE SOUP

SERVES 6 TO 8

3- to 4-pound
whole chicken

3 large carrots, cut into
¼-inch slices

1 medium onion, chopped

3 celery stalks, cut into
¼-inch slices

2 quarts chicken stock,
homemade (page 104) or
store-bought

2 teaspoons Stone House
Seasoning (page 226)

1 teaspoon fresh thyme
leaves or ½ teaspoon dried

1 bay leaf

2½ cups wide egg noodles

Grandmother Verdie swore that homemade chicken soup was the cure for the common cold, and she would slowly simmer her soup all day on the stove if she heard a hint of a sneeze. I was never one to disagree with her, but I make mine in the slow cooker, which is a whole lot easier. I love it even when no one in my house has the sniffles!

1   Put the chicken, carrots, onion, celery, chicken stock, seasoning mix, thyme, and bay leaf in a 6-quart slow cooker. Cover and cook on low for 8 hours.

2   Remove the bay leaf and discard. Remove the chicken from the slow cooker. When it's cool enough to handle, shred the meat and return it to the slow cooker. Add the noodles.

3   Cover and cook on low, checking after 3 minutes, until the noodles are just tender. Serve.

southern hospitality
Ladle chicken soup into a Mason jar and take to a friend who is feeling under the weather. There's nothing like homemade chicken soup to make you feel better!

freezer friendly
Prepare the soup without adding the noodles and let cool completely. Pour into freezer bags, removing as much air as possible as you seal. Freeze for up to 3 months. To serve, thaw in the refrigerator overnight. Pour the soup into a saucepan set over medium heat and reheat until warmed through, about 20 minutes. Meanwhile, cook the noodles in another saucepan according to the package directions, and stir them into the soup for serving.

SLOW COOKER HOPPIN' JOHN SOUP

SERVES 6 TO 8

1 pound dried black-eyed peas, rinsed, soaked overnight, and drained

3 cups chopped turnip greens

1 medium onion, chopped

3 carrots, chopped

3 celery stalks, chopped

6 cups chicken stock, homemade (page 104) or store-bought

2 teaspoons Stone House Seasoning (page 226)

1 ham bone or about 5 strips of thick-sliced bacon

2 cups cooked long-grain rice (see page 92)

Black-eyed peas, turnip greens, and pork are staples for a Southern New Year, and this soup is a wonderful way to bring them all together in one delicious bowl. I love that I can toss everything in the slow cooker and then stir in cooked rice when ready to serve. I don't know about you, but I think that is lucky indeed! Serve with hot sauce, Pepper Jelly (page 220), or Chow Chow (page 230) and a slice of cornbread for a perfect meal to ring in the New Year!

1   Combine the black-eyed peas, turnip greens, onion, carrots, celery, chicken stock, and house seasoning in a 6-quart slow cooker. Add the ham bone.

2   Cover and cook on high for about 8 hours, or until the peas are tender.

3   Remove and discard the ham bone, leaving any bits of ham that may have cooked into the soup. (If you used bacon, remove and discard.) Stir in the rice and serve.

southern hospitality

New Year's Day is a perfect occasion for extending a little hospitality! Invite family and friends over for a Lucky Lunch of this Hoppin' John Soup, cornbread, Sweet Tea Concentrate (page 222), and Mama's Cream Cheese Pound Cake (page 210).

freezer friendly

Let the cooked soup cool completely. Pour into freezer bags, removing as much air as possible as you seal. Freeze for up to 3 months. To serve, thaw in the refrigerator overnight. Pour the soup into a saucepan set over medium heat. Reheat until warmed through, 10 to 15 minutes. If the soup is too thick, add a little water.

GRAND-MOTHER'S CHICKEN *and* DUMPLINGS

SERVES 8

3½-pound whole chicken

1½ teaspoons kosher salt

Grandmother Earlene's Biscuits dough (page 174)

6 tablespoons salted butter

2 cups whole milk

½ teaspoon freshly ground black pepper

Chopped parsley

Growing up, whenever Grandmother Verdie said she was making her chicken and dumplings, my sister, Wendy, and I would beg to eat supper with her. Her recipe is a prize—thick and creamy, and full of tender chicken and dumplings that are light as a feather. So light, in fact, that my son called it cloud soup when he was a little bitty fella. I've reduced the amount of butter from Grandmother's original recipe, but it's still just as delicious!

1   Put the chicken in a Dutch oven and cover with water by about 3 inches. Bring to a boil over high heat, then reduce the heat to low and cook until the chicken is very tender, about 2 hours.

2   Remove the chicken from the broth. When it's cool enough to handle, pull the meat off the bone in strips, returning only the meat to the broth. Add the salt to the broth and bring to a boil.

3   Put the biscuit dough on lightly floured paper towels and roll about ¼ inch thick. Cut the dough into 1-inch strips and then pinch off 1½-inch-long pieces. Drop the dough pieces into the boiling broth. Stir after every few additions of dough to make sure they are submerged in the broth.

4   Add the butter and milk. Let boil gently, stirring occasionally, until the dumplings are completely cooked, 3 to 5 minutes. Remove a dumpling and cut it in half to test for doneness, if needed. Remove the pan from the heat and top with freshly ground black pepper and garnish with parsley for serving.

NOT JUST GAME DAY CHILI

SERVES 6 TO 8

1 pound ground beef

1 medium onion, chopped

3 tablespoons Espresso Chili Spice Blend (page 227), plus more for serving

2 teaspoons Stone House Seasoning (page 226)

1 teaspoon Worcestershire sauce

2 cups tomato sauce, homemade (page 229) or 2½ cups store-bought

2 medium plum tomatoes, chopped

2 cups cooked (see page 38) or drained canned navy, black, or pinto beans

Optional toppings: sour cream, grated Cheddar cheese, sliced radishes

Chili and football go hand in hand. Traditionally, I've always started the chili in the morning so that it can simmer and simmer before the game starts later in the afternoon or evening. But I've discovered that chili doesn't have to simmer all day to be packed with amazing flavor. This recipe is proof! The key is adding a good dose of seasonings early in the cooking process; then the chili is ready in no time.

In a Dutch oven set over medium heat, cook the ground beef and onion, breaking up the meat with a wooden spoon, until browned through, 3 to 5 minutes. Stir in the chili spice blend, house seasoning, and Worcestershire sauce and cook until fragrant, about 1 minute. Stir in the tomato sauce, tomatoes, and beans and simmer until thick, about 15 minutes. Serve with toppings, if desired.

leftover makeover

CHILI-STUFFED POTATOES

Set 4 to 6 Yukon or Idaho baking potatoes on squares of parchment paper or foil. Drizzle with olive oil and sprinkle with salt. Wrap each potato in the parchment or foil and put in a slow cooker. Cover and cook on low for 8 hours. Reheat the chili in a saucepan over medium heat or in a microwave-safe bowl in the microwave until warmed through. Split open the cooked potatoes, loosen the flesh with a fork, and ladle chili on top. Serve with grated Cheddar cheese and yogurt or sour cream, if desired.

freezer friendly

Let the cooked chili cool completely. Pour into freezer bags, removing as much air as possible as you seal. Freeze for up to 3 months. To serve, thaw in the refrigerator overnight. Pour into a saucepan set over medium heat. Reheat until warmed through, 10 to 15 minutes. If the chili is too thick, add a little water.

BROCCOLI PINEAPPLE SALAD

SERVES 6 TO 8

6 cups fresh broccoli florets

1 cup grated Cheddar cheese

½ medium red onion, chopped

1 cup red seedless grapes, halved

½ cup diced fresh pineapple

¼ cup chopped pecans

3 slices of cooked bacon, chopped

1 cup mayonnaise or Greek yogurt

2 tablespoons apple cider vinegar

1 tablespoon sugar

I always think of this salad during the summer when I'm planning cookouts, picnics, and camping trips because it is so well loved and can easily be made ahead. But you can of course serve it any time of year. I've updated this classic Southern recipe by reducing the amount of sugar in the dressing so there's just enough to highlight the sweetness of the grapes and pineapple.

1   In a large bowl, combine the broccoli, cheese, onion, grapes, pineapple, pecans, and bacon.

2   In a small bowl, combine the mayonnaise, vinegar, and sugar. Spoon the dressing over the broccoli mixture and toss gently until evenly coated.

POPPY SEED FRUIT SALAD

SERVES 6 TO 8

8 cups mixed cubed fresh fruit (my favorite mixture includes pineapple, apples, berries, oranges, and grapes)

3 tablespoons fresh orange juice

3 tablespoons honey

1 tablespoon fresh lemon juice

2 tablespoons sugar

1 teaspoon poppy seeds

½ teaspoon grated fresh ginger or ¼ teaspoon ground

Fruit salad has always been a favorite in my family. I could always count on Mama's making it on the weekends throughout the summer when I was a kid. Now, though, I love to make it year-round. It uses a variety of fresh fruits, which you can mix and match as you like. The flavorful dressing is a little sweet with a zing of ginger. If your fruit is very ripe, you can probably use less honey.

1   Put the fruit in a large bowl.

2   In a Mason jar, combine the orange juice, honey, lemon juice, sugar, poppy seeds, and ginger. Shake well. (You can also whisk the dressing in a small bowl.) Pour half of the dressing over the fruit and toss. Drizzle the remaining dressing over the top and serve immediately.

APPLE RAISIN SLAW

SERVES 6

2 apples, julienned

2 tablespoons pineapple or lemon juice

1 carrot, cut into matchsticks

½ cup raisins

2½ tablespoons mayonnaise or Greek yogurt

1½ tablespoons apple cider vinegar

2 teaspoons stone-ground Dijon mustard

¼ teaspoon kosher salt

My father-in-law, Bob, passed along his slaw adoration to his baby boy, my husband. Bart absolutely loves any kind of slaw, from carrot to broccoli to this apple raisin version. I particularly like the combination of sweet and tangy flavors in this recipe, which is perfect served with Sticky Molasses BBQ Ribs (page 86).

1   In a large bowl, toss the apples with the pineapple juice to coat well. Add the carrot and raisins.

2   In a small bowl, whisk together the mayonnaise, vinegar, mustard, and salt. Pour the dressing over the apple mixture and toss well.

HEIRLOOM TOMATO SALAD *with* CHARRED CORN *and* OKRA

SERVES 6 TO 8

2 ears fresh or frozen and thawed corn

½ pound fresh or frozen and thawed okra

3 heirloom tomatoes, cut into ¼-inch slices

5 or 6 scallions, chopped

Kosher salt and freshly ground black pepper

Pepper Jelly Vinaigrette (recipe at right)

They say that we eat first with our eyes. If so, get ready to feast your eyes on this salad! Arranged on a large platter, it is absolutely gorgeous. I'm lucky that I get to make this salad with vegetables picked fresh from my garden—the flavors are just so vibrant! Seek out the best veggies you can find from a farmer's market or CSA to make this dish sing. However, you can also use frozen corn and okra, if you've missed them at their prime.

1 Cut the kernels off the cobs and set aside. Slice the okra lengthwise in half and set aside.

2 Heat two 10- to 12-inch skillets over medium-high heat. Put the corn kernels in one skillet and the sliced okra in the other. Cook, stirring frequently, until both are charred, about 10 minutes.

3 Arrange the tomato slices on a serving platter and top with the corn, okra, and scallions. Season with salt and pepper to taste. Drizzle some pepper jelly vinaigrette on top and serve extra on the side.

PEPPER JELLY VINAIGRETTE

MAKES ABOUT 1 CUP

¾ cup olive oil

¼ cup white vinegar

3 tablespoons pepper jelly, homemade (page 220) or store-bought

1 tablespoon Dijon mustard

1 garlic clove, minced, or ⅛ teaspoon garlic powder

½ teaspoon kosher salt

¼ teaspoon freshly ground black pepper

In a Mason jar, combine the oil, vinegar, pepper jelly, mustard, garlic, salt, and pepper. Secure the lid tightly and shake vigorously until well combined. The dressing will keep in the refrigerator for 3 days if you use fresh garlic, or 2 weeks if you use garlic powder. Shake well before serving.

GRILLED WATERMELON *and* PEACH SALAD *with* BASIL *and* FETA

SERVES 6

1 tablespoon olive oil

8 watermelon wedges, about 1 inch thick and 4 inches wide

2 medium ripe peaches, peeled and cut into wedges

½ teaspoon kosher salt

2 tablespoons roughly chopped fresh basil

1 (4-ounce) package feta cheese, crumbled

2 tablespoons honey

Balsamic Reduction (page 32)

Grilling the watermelon and peaches releases even more of their natural sweetness, while giving them a hint of smoke from the fire. Combining them with creamy feta, bright basil, and a drizzle of balsamic reduction makes this one magical salad. It is also mighty nice to make in the dead heat of a Southern summer, since the grill does the work (a grill pan works in a pinch too!).

1 Preheat a grill to medium or set a grill pan over medium heat.

2 Brush the grates with olive oil. Arrange the watermelon and peach slices on the grill and sprinkle with ¼ teaspoon of the salt. Grill until there are grill marks on the fruit and it just begins to soften, about 3 minutes. Flip the fruit and sprinkle with the remaining ¼ teaspoon salt and grill the second side, about 3 more minutes.

3 Transfer the fruit to a platter and top with the basil and feta. Drizzle with the honey and balsamic reduction, and serve.

SPRING ARUGULA, RADISH, *and* PEA SALAD

SERVES 4 TO 6

3 cups packed fresh arugula

2 cups packed fresh spring
lettuce greens

6 medium radishes,
thinly sliced

½ cup snap peas, ends
trimmed, cut into
1-inch pieces

5 green onions, cut into
1-inch pieces

1 (4-ounce) package
mozzarella cheese, cut into
2-inch pieces

¼ cup Mint and Parsley
Pesto (page 122)

2 tablespoons
red wine vinegar

1 tablespoon Dijon mustard

½ cup olive oil

This salad and vinaigrette include many of my favorites from the spring garden—peppery arugula, tender spring lettuce, crunchy radishes, sweet peas, and fragrant mint and parsley. The combination is incredibly flavorful, but not in an overpowering way. I love to serve this salad with the Chicken and Snap Pea Skewers (page 120), but you'll find that this salad goes great with fish and shrimp too!

1 Toss the arugula, lettuce, radishes, snap peas, green onions, and mozzarella together in a large bowl.

2 In a small bowl, whisk together the pesto, vinegar, mustard, and olive oil. Drizzle over the salad, toss gently, and serve.

BISCUITS
& BREADS

GRAND-MOTHER EARLENE'S BISCUITS

MAKES 12 BISCUITS

2¼ cups all-purpose flour, plus more for dusting

2 teaspoons baking powder

Pinch of kosher salt

6 tablespoons cold salted butter, diced, plus 1 tablespoon melted salted butter, for brushing

¾ to 1 cup cold buttermilk

I learned early that biscuits are the little black dress of Southern foods. They're perfect for every occasion, from breakfast to a weeknight meal to a celebratory dinner. It seems everyone has their own special way of making them. My Grandmother Earlene worked her dough by hand and then pinched off her biscuits, rolled them in a bit of flour, and tenderly placed them in her pan. I love to use this pinch method, though I also describe how to roll them out and cut them with a biscuit cutter, which lets the biscuits rise even more.

1   Preheat the oven to 475°F.

2   In a large bowl, whisk together the flour, baking powder, and salt. Using your fingers, work the pieces of cold butter into the flour mixture until the butter is the size of peas. Make a well in the center of the mixture and pour in the ¾ cup buttermilk. Working from the sides of the bowl, pull the flour into the buttermilk until the mixture is just combined, taking care not to overwork the dough. Use up to ¼ cup more buttermilk if needed; the dough will be a little sticky.

3   Place flour for dusting on a pastry cloth or paper towel and dust your hands lightly with flour. Gently pull the edges together to form a large ball. Turn the ball of dough over once to lightly dust it with flour so it's easier to handle. For each biscuit, pinch off a piece of dough about the size of a large egg and gently shape it into a ball about 2 inches in diameter. Place the biscuits on a lightly buttered baking sheet or in two 9-inch cake pans. Gently pat each biscuit to flatten the top slightly. They should be about 1 inch tall and placed shoulder to shoulder for a better rise.

4   Bake until light golden brown, 10 to 12 minutes. Brush the tops with the melted butter and serve warm.

(recipe continues)

even easier!

If you prefer to cut out your biscuits rather than shape them by hand, here's how to do it. Gently pat the dough into a rectangle and then fold one side of the rectangle to the center of the dough. Repeat with all four sides. Lightly dust a rolling pin with flour and roll the dough 1 inch thick. Using a sharp 2-inch cutter, press straight down onto the dough and lift up, being careful not to twist the cutter. Place the biscuits on a lightly buttered baking sheet, sides touching. Bake and brush with melted butter as directed for hand-shaped biscuits.

freezer friendly

Shape the biscuits but don't bake them. Place them on a parchment-lined baking sheet, wrap well with plastic wrap, and flash freeze until fully frozen, 15 to 20 minutes. Transfer the biscuits to a freezer bag and freeze for up to 7 months. To bake, place the frozen biscuits on a baking sheet and bake according to the recipe, adding a few minutes if needed, until golden brown. Remove from the oven and brush with melted butter.

PIMENTO CHEESE BISCUITS

MAKES 12 BISCUITS

Oil mister or cooking spray

2 cups self-rising flour

½ teaspoon freshly ground black pepper

¼ teaspoon cayenne pepper

3 tablespoons mayonnaise

1 cup buttermilk

1½ cups shredded sharp Cheddar cheese

¼ cup diced pimentos, drained

1 tablespoon salted butter, melted, for brushing

Oh my goodness, how I adore these biscuits. They were inspired by my love of toasting day-old biscuits and spreading a little bit of pimento cheese on them. I thought it might work well to combine the two ideas, and, well, it worked out great! Serve them with my Heirloom Tomato Salad with Charred Corn and Okra (page 166) or with soup for a filling lunch or light supper.

1   Preheat the oven to 475°F. Lightly spray a rimmed baking sheet with oil.

2   In a large bowl, whisk together the flour, black pepper, and cayenne pepper. Stir in the mayonnaise and buttermilk until the dough just comes together. Fold in the cheese and pimentos. Scoop heaping tablespoons of the dough onto the prepared baking sheet.

3   Bake until golden brown, 10 to 12 minutes. Brush with the melted butter and serve warm.

freezer friendly

Let the baked biscuits cool completely. Wrap the baking sheet well with plastic wrap and flash freeze for 15 to 20 minutes. Transfer to a freezer bag and freeze for up to 3 months. To serve, place frozen biscuits on a baking sheet and reheat in a 350°F oven until warm, about 8 minutes.

even easier!
Prepare the dough without any filling and cut biscuits with a 2-inch cutter. Place in the prepared skillet. Mix the melted butter, garlic, Parmesan cheese, and parsley and brush on the tops of the biscuits. Bake for 10 to 12 minutes, until lightly browned.

PARMESAN GARLIC BISCUIT ROLLS

MAKES 12 ROLLS

2 teaspoons olive oil

2 cups self-rising flour, plus more for dusting

1½ cups heavy cream

2 tablespoons salted butter, melted

1½ cups freshly grated Parmesan cheese

3 garlic cloves, minced

¼ cup chopped fresh parsley

No one will ever guess how easy these biscuit rolls are to make. You simply layer melted butter, Parmesan cheese, garlic, and fresh parsley onto biscuit dough; roll it into a large cylinder; and slice the dough to form the biscuit rolls, or pinwheels. Then nestle them into a skillet and bake until golden brown. Yum! They are delicious with Easy Skillet Lasagna (page 74) or alongside a soup or salad.

1 Preheat the oven to 475°F. Grease a 12-inch ovenproof skillet with the olive oil.

2 Put the flour in a medium bowl and make a well in the center. Pour the cream into the well. Using a wooden spoon and working from the sides of the bowl, stir the flour into the cream until the mixture is just combined, taking care not to overwork the dough.

3 Dust a pastry cloth or paper towels and your hands lightly with flour. Turn the dough out onto the floured cloth and gently pull it into a large ball. Lightly press to flatten it to about ½ inch thick. Fold the dough from each side toward the center, repeating on all four sides. Lightly flour a rolling pin and roll the dough ½ inch thick, or just pat it out with your hands.

4 Brush 1 tablespoon of the melted butter over the dough. Sprinkle with the Parmesan, garlic, and parsley. Working from one side of the dough, roll tightly until you have a log. Cut into 1½-inch slices and place in the prepared skillet (the sides will be touching). Drizzle the remaining tablespoon of melted butter over the biscuits.

5 Bake until lightly browned, 10 to 12 minutes.

freezer friendly

Let the baked biscuits cool completely. Wrap the baking sheet well with plastic wrap and flash freeze for 15 to 20 minutes. Transfer to a freezer bag and freeze for up to 3 months. To serve, put the frozen biscuits on a baking sheet and reheat in a 350°F oven until warm, about 15 minutes.

SAUSAGE *and* CHEDDAR SPOON BREAD

SERVES 8

Oil mister or cooking spray

1 pound breakfast sausage, crumbled

½ medium onion, finely chopped

3½ cups whole milk

2 tablespoons salted butter

1½ cups fine yellow cornmeal

5 large eggs, beaten

1½ cups grated Cheddar cheese

Is it bread? Is it a soufflé? A side dish? A main? Well . . . yes! No matter how you categorize it, spoon bread is very Southern and very delicious! There are many types of spoon breads, the most basic having nothing but a nice cornmeal taste. This sausage and Cheddar version has plenty of flavor, even with less butter than traditional recipes and no sugar. You won't miss either!

1 Preheat the oven to 400°F. Lightly spray a 9 × 13-inch baking dish with oil.

2 In a medium skillet set over medium heat, cook the sausage, breaking up the meat with a wooden spoon, until it begins to render its fat, about 3 minutes. Add the onion and cook, stirring, until the onion is soft and translucent and the sausage has browned, 3 to 5 minutes. Using a slotted spoon, transfer the sausage and onion to a large bowl.

3 In a 3-quart saucepan set over medium-low heat, bring the milk and butter to a simmer. Whisk in the cornmeal and cook, whisking constantly to prevent any lumps from forming, until thickened, 3 to 5 minutes. Pour the cornmeal into the bowl with the sausage and onion. Stir well. Let cool completely, about 10 minutes.

4 Fold the eggs and cheese into the cooled cornmeal mixture and pour it all into the prepared baking dish.

5 Bake until puffy, lightly browned, and set completely in the middle, about 30 minutes.

even easier!
Omit the sausage and onion from this spoon bread recipe for a classic version that works well with any main dish!

BOOTS BUTLER'S YEAST ROLLS

SERVES 6 TO 8

1 cup lukewarm (100°F to 110°F) whole milk

2 tablespoons sugar

2¼ teaspoons (1 packet) active dry yeast

1 large egg

2 teaspoons kosher salt

4 tablespoons (½ stick) salted butter, melted and cooled, plus 1 tablespoon melted, for brushing

4½ cups all-purpose flour

Olive oil

My mother and her best friend share the same name: Judy. This friend's mother, affectionately called Boots, is the epitome of a Southern lady. She lives in a nearby town in Alabama, right over the state line. Her yeast rolls are the best I've ever tasted—I just didn't know they were hers! I had always thought they were my grandmother's, until after she passed away and we were going through her kitchen; we found the recipe for the rolls on the back of an envelope with "Boots Butler's Yeast Rolls" scrawled across the top! Turns out Boots's recipe had been passed to my grandmother by a relative of Boots with whom Grandmother worked when my mama was in high school, which was well before Mama and her friend Judy met. Just think, all this time, the two Judys' connection went even further than their names and friendship—they were also connected by these rolls!

1 In the bowl of a stand mixer, combine the milk, sugar, and yeast. Let sit until the yeast begins to foam, about 3 minutes. Fit the mixer with the paddle attachment and add the egg, salt, 4 tablespoons butter, and add ½ cup of the flour at a time until the dough comes together in a ball that can be easily handled, 6 to 8 minutes. (You can knead by hand for 20 minutes.) Cover with a clean cloth and set in a warm place, not exceeding 90°F, free of drafts to rise until doubled in bulk, about 1 hour.

2 Grease 2 round cake pans or 1 rimmed baking sheet with olive oil. Grease a work surface with a little olive oil.

3 Punch the dough down, turn it out onto the greased surface, and knead until smooth, about 3 minutes. Divide the dough into 16 equal pieces and place them in the prepared pan(s). Cover the rolls with a clean cloth and set in a warm place, not exceeding 100°F, and let rise until doubled in bulk, about 1 hour. To test if the rolls are ready for baking, press your finger gently into the side of the dough. If the indentation into the dough remains, it is ready for baking.

4 Preheat the oven to 425°F.

5 Brush the tops of the rolls with the remaining 1 tablespoon melted butter. Bake until golden brown, 12 to 15 minutes.

freezer friendly
Arrange the uncooked rolls in round, disposable cake pans and wrap well with plastic and then with foil. Freeze for up to 7 months. To serve, thaw in the refrigerator overnight. Unwrap, brush with melted butter, and bake according to the recipe instructions, adding a few minutes, if needed, to get them golden brown.

POPOVERS

MAKES 12 POPOVERS

Oil mister or cooking spray

3 tablespoons salted
butter, melted

1 cup all-purpose flour

½ teaspoon kosher salt

3 large eggs, beaten

1 cup whole milk

When Bart and I first married, I asked him if he could have any meal in the world, what it would be. After a few minutes, he said, "Roast beef and popovers." That was over twenty years ago, but I still make it for him to this day. There is no need to buy a special popover pan; a muffin tin works just fine. They couldn't be easier! (And don't miss my Balsamic Beef on page 90.)

1   Arrange one rack in the lower third of your oven and remove any other racks. Preheat the oven to 450°F. Lightly spray a muffin tin with oil. Pour ½ teaspoon of the melted butter into each cup of the muffin tin.

2   In a large bowl, whisk together the flour and salt.

3   In a separate large bowl, whisk together the remaining 1 tablespoon butter, the eggs, and milk until well combined and light in color, about 3 minutes. Whisking constantly, slowly pour the egg mixture into the flour mixture. Pour the batter into the prepared muffin tin, filling each cup halfway.

4   Bake for 10 minutes. Reduce the oven temperature to 325°F and bake until golden brown and puffed, 10 more minutes. Serve immediately.

BART'S CINNAMON ROLLS

MAKES 24 ROLLS

dough

1 cup warm milk

½ cup granulated sugar

2¼ teaspoons (1 packet) active dry yeast

4½ cups all-purpose flour, plus more for dusting

8 tablespoons (1 stick) salted butter, melted, plus more for greasing the bowl and baking sheet

2 large eggs

2 teaspoons kosher salt

filling

8 tablespoons (1 stick) salted butter, softened

1 cup packed dark brown sugar

2½ tablespoons ground cinnamon

frosting

1½ cups confectioners' sugar

8 tablespoons (1 stick) butter, softened

¼ cup cream cheese

1½ teaspoons vanilla extract

⅛ teaspoon kosher salt

Bart based his recipe on the one his mother makes every Christmas. They are a little lighter in sugar and are foolproof! He and Sam have taken up the tradition at our house because—did you know?—Santa prefers cinnamon rolls!

1 **Make the dough:** In a large bowl, combine the milk, sugar, and yeast. Let sit until foamy, about 3 minutes. Stir in the flour, butter, eggs, and salt.

2 Butter a large glass bowl. Turn the dough onto a lightly floured work surface and knead until smooth, 10 to 12 minutes. Form the dough into a ball and put it in the bowl. Turn the dough over once to grease all over. Cover lightly with plastic or a clean dish towel and place in a warm location. Let rise until doubled in size, about 60 minutes.

3 **Roll and fill the dough:** Put the dough on a lightly floured work surface and roll it out ¼ inch thick. Spread the softened butter over the top of the dough.

4 Lightly butter a baking sheet. In a small bowl, stir together the brown sugar and cinnamon and sprinkle all over the dough. Beginning at a long end, tightly roll the dough into a log. Cut the dough into ¾- to 1-inch slices and place side by side on the baking sheet. Let rise until doubled in size, 30 minutes.

5 While the rolls rise, preheat the oven to 400°F.

6 Bake until lightly browned, 15 to 20 minutes. Let cool slightly.

7 **Meanwhile, make the frosting:** In a stand mixer fitted with the whisk attachment, beat together the confectioners' sugar, butter, cream cheese, vanilla, and salt. Frost the warm cinnamon rolls.

freezer friendly

Let the baked rolls cool completely, then wrap well with plastic wrap and foil. To serve, thaw in the refrigerator overnight, remove both wraps, and reheat in a 300°F oven for about 10 minutes until warmed through. Then, frost while still warm and serve.

SWEET ENDINGS

LULU BELLE'S LEMON MERINGUE PIE

SERVES 8

1 cup whole milk

1 cup granulated sugar

¼ cup cornstarch

⅛ teaspoon kosher salt

4 large egg yolks
(reserve the whites for
the meringue)

4 tablespoons (½ stick)
salted butter

¼ cup fresh lemon juice

1 cup sour cream

1 Perfect Piecrust, prebaked
and cooled (page 100)

Mile-High Meringue
(recipe follows)

Aunt Lulu Belle and Uncle James's property adjoined ours, and there was a well-worn path between our two backyards. Her boys, Jeff and Mark, were older than my sister and me, but they were still our favorite playmates when we were young. While we played, Lulu Belle was always busy in the kitchen cooking, putting up fruits and vegetables from their garden, and trying her best to just keep track of us all. Her pies have always been legendary in our family and this lemon meringue is a favorite. I've updated her recipe to use butter instead of margarine, and I love it even more!

1 Preheat the oven to 375°F.

2 In a large saucepan set over medium heat, combine the milk, sugar, cornstarch, and salt. Cook, whisking constantly, until the mixture begins to boil and becomes very thick, about 12 minutes.

3 In a small bowl, whisk the egg yolks. Pour about ½ cup of the hot milk mixture into the egg yolks and whisk thoroughly. Pour all of the egg mixture back into the milk mixture and cook, whisking constantly, until it begins to boil, about 3 minutes. Cook until the filling is thick and coats the back of a wooden spoon, 2 more minutes. Remove the pan from the heat and stir in the butter and lemon juice. Fold in the sour cream. Pour the filling into the prepared pie shell. Cover the filling with the meringue, making sure to spread it all the way to the edges of the crust.

4 Bake until the meringue is golden brown, about 10 minutes. Transfer the pie to a wire rack and let cool to room temperature. Refrigerate until cool, for at least 1 hour, before serving.

(recipe continues)

MILE-HIGH MERINGUE

MAKES ENOUGH FOR ONE 9-INCH PIE

4 large egg whites

½ teaspoon cream of tartar

¼ cup confectioners' sugar

In the bowl of a stand mixer fitted with the whisk attachment (or using a hand mixer), beat the egg whites until foamy, about 1 minute. Beat in the cream of tartar. Slowly add the sugar, 1 tablespoon at a time, beating after each addition until the sugar dissolves. Continue beating until the egg whites form stiff peaks, about 6 minutes.

GERMAN CHOCOLATE CAKE

SERVES 12

Baking spray

2 cups all-purpose flour

2 cups sugar

¾ cup unsweetened cocoa powder

2 teaspoons baking powder

1½ teaspoons baking soda

1 teaspoon kosher salt

1 teaspoon espresso powder

1 cup whole milk

2 large eggs

2 teaspoons vanilla extract

½ cup coconut oil, melted, or canola oil

1 cup boiling water

Coconut Pecan Frosting (recipe follows)

One of the most popular recipes on my website is my chocolate cake. I took that favorite recipe and turned it into this oh-so-delicious version! A few notes on this cake: The espresso powder intensifies the chocolate flavor, making this cake taste even more chocolaty. I can usually find it at my grocery store, and it's available at cooking and baking supply stores and online. I've also had my local coffee shop finely grind espresso into a powder for me. It does not add a heavy coffee flavor, and it's fine to omit, if you can't find it. I also added the option of using melted coconut oil to deepen the coconut flavor. Note that the cake batter will be very thin after adding the boiling water. Don't fret; it will result in a most delightful cake!

1 Preheat the oven to 350°F. Prepare two 9-inch cake pans by spraying with baking spray or buttering and lightly flouring them.

2 In the clean bowl of a stand mixer fitted with the whisk attachment (or using a hand mixer), combine the flour, sugar, cocoa, baking powder, baking soda, salt, and espresso powder. Add the milk, eggs, and vanilla and beat on medium speed until well combined. Reduce the speed to low and add the coconut oil. With the mixer still on low speed, carefully and slowly pour in the boiling water and beat until well combined, about 3 minutes. Pour the batter into the prepared cake pans.

3 Bake until a wooden toothpick inserted in the center comes out clean, 30 to 35 minutes. Let the cakes cool for 10 minutes. Turn the cakes out of the pans onto wire racks and let cool completely before frosting.

4 Spread the frosting on the top of one of the cake layers. Top with the second layer and frost the top only.

(recipe continues)

COCONUT PECAN FROSTING

MAKES 3 CUPS

3 large egg yolks

1¼ cups evaporated milk, homemade (see sidebar)
or store-bought

2 cups granulated sugar

8 tablespoons (1 stick) salted butter, at room temperature

1½ teaspoons vanilla extract

2 cups sweetened flaked coconut

1 cup chopped pecans, toasted (see page 82)

1   In a medium bowl, beat together the egg yolks and evaporated
    milk and pour the mixture into a large saucepan. Add the sugar
    and stir until dissolved. Add the butter, set the pan over low
    heat, and cook, stirring constantly, until thick, 10 to 12 minutes.

2   Remove the pan from the heat and add the vanilla, coconut, and
    pecans. Stir with a wooden spoon until thickened to a spreading
    consistency, about 5 minutes. Spread on the cake while the
    frosting is still warm.

HOMEMADE EVAPORATED MILK

Bring 2½ cups whole milk to a low simmer in a medium saucepan
set over medium-low heat. Cook, whisking constantly, until reduced
by half, about 30 minutes. Let cool completely. Store in an airtight
container in the refrigerator for up to a week.

ITALIAN CREAM CAKE

**MAKES ONE
3-TIERED, 8-INCH
LAYER CAKE;
SERVES 12**

cake

Baking spray

5 large eggs, separated

16 tablespoons (2 sticks)
salted butter, at room
temperature

2 cups granulated sugar

2 cups all-purpose flour

1 teaspoon baking soda

1 cup buttermilk

1 teaspoon vanilla extract

1 cup sweetened
flaked coconut

1 cup chopped pecans

frosting

16 tablespoons (2 sticks)
salted butter, at room
temperature

2 (8-ounce) packages
cream cheese, at room
temperature

4 cups confectioners'
sugar, sifted

1 teaspoon vanilla extract

1 cup chopped pecans

My wedding cake was a multitiered confection of Italian cream cake with cream cheese frosting and satellite cakes surrounding it. Mama had been making it for special occasions in our family ever since I could remember, and I knew it was just what I wanted for our big day. I've updated her recipe to include my technique for the frosting, which makes it light, airy, and absolutely delicious!

1   Preheat the oven to 350°F. Prepare three 8-inch cake pans by spraying with baking spray or buttering and lightly flouring them.

2   For the cake: In the bowl of a stand mixer fitted with the whisk attachment (or using a hand mixer), beat the egg whites until they hold a stiff peak, about 7 minutes.

3   In a clean bowl of a stand mixer fitted with the paddle attachment (or using a hand mixer), beat the butter and sugar at medium speed until light and fluffy, about 5 minutes. Add the egg yolks one at a time, beating after each addition until combined.

4   In a medium bowl, whisk together the flour and baking soda. Alternate adding the flour mixture and the buttermilk to the butter and sugar mixture, beating after each addition until just blended. Stir in the vanilla, coconut, and pecans. Fold in the whipped egg whites. Divide the batter among the prepared pans.

5   Bake until the center of the cake springs back to the touch and a wooden toothpick inserted in the center comes out clean, about 30 minutes. Let the cakes cool for 10 minutes. Turn the cakes out of the pans onto wire racks and let cool before frosting.

6   For the frosting: In the bowl of a stand mixer fitted with the whisk attachment (or using a hand mixer), beat the butter and cream cheese at medium speed until light and fluffy, about 5 minutes. Add the sugar, 1 cup at a time, beating at the highest speed for about 10 seconds after each addition. Stir in the vanilla and nuts.

7   Spread the frosting over the top of one of the cooled cake layers. Add a second cake layer and spread with frosting. Top with the remaining cake layer and frost the top and sides of the cake. Because of the cream cheese in the frosting, this cake needs to be refrigerated.

freezer friendly
Let the baked cake layers cool completely. Wrap them well with plastic wrap and then with foil. Put each layer into a freezer bag and freeze for up to 2 months. To serve, thaw in the refrigerator overnight. The next day, the layers are ready to fill and frost.

STRAWBERRY SHORTCAKES *with* SWEET CREAM CHEESE BISCUITS

SERVES 6

1 pint fresh strawberries, hulled and quartered

¼ cup sugar

2 cups self-rising flour, plus more for dusting

Pinch of kosher salt

4 ounces cream cheese, at room temperature, cut into chunks

5 tablespoons frozen salted butter, grated

½ cup whole milk

Perfect Whipped Cream (recipe follows)

There is nothing like strawberry shortcakes in the height of strawberry season. I make mine with sweet biscuits that have a little bit of cream cheese in them. They make a tender and creamy biscuit that works well for sweet treats. Strawberries out of season? Then by all means try the cinnamon apple variation. I think you'll love them as much as we do!

1 Preheat the oven to 475°F.

2 In a small bowl, toss together the strawberries and 2 tablespoons of the sugar. Refrigerate while you make the biscuits and whipped cream.

3 In a medium bowl, combine the remaining 2 tablespoons sugar, the flour, salt, cream cheese, and butter with a pastry blender. Pour in the milk and stir until just well combined.

4 Dust a pastry cloth or paper towels lightly with flour. Turn the dough out onto the floured cloth and knead gently until smooth, about 3 turns. Fold each side of the dough into the center. Lightly flour a rolling pin and roll the dough ½ inch thick. Cut out rounds using a sharp 3-inch cutter, taking care not to twist the cutter. Place the biscuits on an ungreased rimmed baking sheet.

5 Bake until light golden brown, 10 to 12 minutes.

6 To assemble, split open the biscuits. Top the bottom halves with the strawberries and some of their juices and a dollop of whipped cream. Place a biscuit top on each stack and repeat the layering of the strawberries, strawberry juices, and a final dollop of whipped cream. Spoon more strawberry juices over the whipped cream and serve.

(recipe continues)

PERFECT WHIPPED CREAM

MAKES 2 CUPS

1 cup cold whipping cream

2 tablespoons confectioners' sugar

½ teaspoon vanilla extract

1   Put the bowl and whisk attachment of a stand mixer in the freezer for 15 minutes before whipping the cream.

2   In the cold bowl of a stand mixer fitted with the cold whisk attachment (or using a hand mixer), beat the cream, sugar, and vanilla, beginning on low speed and gradually increasing to high speed. Beat until stiff peaks form, being careful not to overmix, about 5 minutes.

CINNAMON APPLE SHORTCAKES

Cut 2 Granny Smith apples into 8 wedges each. Cook the apple wedges and ¼ cup apple butter (page 224) in a medium skillet set over medium heat until the apples are tender, about 10 minutes. Serve with the sweet cream cheese biscuits and whipped cream.

BUTTERMILK PRALINE CHEESECAKE

SERVES 12

shortbread crust

1 tablespoon salted butter, melted

16 tablespoons (2 sticks) salted butter, at room temperature

2 cups all-purpose flour

½ cup confectioners' sugar

½ cup finely chopped pecans

cheesecake filling

2 (8-ounce) packages cream cheese, at room temperature

2 cups ricotta cheese, at room temperature

1¼ cups granulated sugar

4 large eggs, at room temperature

¼ cup all-purpose flour

¼ teaspoon kosher salt

2 teaspoons fresh lemon juice

1½ teaspoons vanilla extract

Cheesecake is my brother-in-law Steve's very favorite dessert. When you ask him what he'd like for his birthday, cheesecake is always the answer. Special occasions? Cheesecake, of course. For this recipe, I combined a bit of his favorite cheesecake (the filling) along with Bart's favorite topping (the buttermilk praline) and Mama's favorite crust (pecan shortbread). If you aren't a huge fan of nuts, just omit them from the crust and the topping and this will still make for a crowd-pleasing dessert. Unless you tell them, they probably won't even guess that you replaced some of the cream cheese with ricotta in this cheesecake.

1   Preheat the oven to 350°F. Brush the melted butter over the bottom and up the sides of a 9-inch springform pan.

2   **Make the crust:** In a medium bowl, beat the softened butter, flour, and confectioners' sugar with an electric mixer. Stir in the pecans. Press the dough into the bottom and 1 inch up the sides of the prepared pan.

3   Bake until light golden brown, 12 to 15 minutes. Remove from the oven, set on a wire rack, and let cool completely.

4   Reduce the oven temperature to 325°F.

5   **Make the filling:** In the bowl of a stand mixer fitted with the paddle attachment (or using a hand mixer), beat the cream cheese and ricotta until smooth, about 3 minutes. Add the sugar and beat until just blended. Add the eggs one at a time, beating well after each addition. Add the flour and salt and beat until just blended. Reduce the mixer speed to low and mix in the lemon juice and vanilla. Let rest for 5 minutes before pouring into the crust.

6   Bake until the edges are set, 1 hour. The middle 2 to 3 inches will still be soft and have a bit of movement. Do not overbake! Do not use a knife or a toothpick to test for doneness. Keep the oven door closed, turn the oven off, and leave the cheesecake in the closed oven for 1 more hour.

(recipe continues)

buttermilk praline topping

1 cup granulated sugar

½ teaspoon baking soda

½ cup buttermilk

8 tablespoons (1 stick) salted butter

½ cup pecans, roughly chopped

1 teaspoon vanilla extract

freezer friendly

Let the cooked (untopped) cheesecake cool completely. Wrap well in plastic wrap, then foil. Store in a freezer bag in the freezer for up to 3 months. To serve, thaw in the refrigerator overnight. Prepare the praline topping, pour it over the cold cheesecake, and return the cheesecake to the refrigerator to allow the topping to cool and harden, about 30 minutes. Remove from the refrigerator about 15 minutes before slicing and serving.

7 Transfer the cheesecake to wire racks. Let cool to room temperature, about 1 hour. Cover the pan with plastic wrap and refrigerate for at least 4 hours and as long as overnight.

8 Remove the cheesecake from the refrigerator and run the tip of a sharp knife around the edges. Release the sides of the springform pan and run a sharp knife under the cake to remove the bottom of the pan. Using a large spatula, place the cheesecake on a serving plate. (At this point, you can wrap it in plastic wrap and refrigerate for up to 5 days before adding the topping.)

9 For the topping: In a medium saucepan set over medium heat, combine the sugar, baking soda, and buttermilk and stir well. Add the butter and cook, stirring constantly, until it reaches the softball stage or a candy thermometer registers 238°F, about 10 minutes. If you do not have a candy thermometer, you can use the cold-water test: Drop a small amount of the topping into a bowl of very cold water. Using your fingers, form the drops into a ball. The ball should flatten easily when removed from the water.

10 Remove the pan from the heat and stir in the pecans and vanilla. Remove the cheesecake from the refrigerator and pour the praline topping over the top. Return the cheesecake to the refrigerator and allow the topping to cool and harden, about 30 minutes. Remove from the refrigerator about 15 minutes before slicing and serving.

even easier!

Sometimes I like to make mini cheesecakes in a muffin tin. They're cute and take a little less time to bake. Put cupcake liners in the cups of a muffin tin and press 1 tablespoon of the crust mixture into the bottoms and up the sides of each. Bake at 350°F until lightly browned, 12 to 15 minutes. Let cool. Reduce the oven temperature to 325°F. Pour the cheesecake filling into the muffin cups, filling them about three-quarters full. Bake for 30 minutes and then leave in the oven for 1 hour with the oven door slightly open. Remove from the oven and let cool to room temperature. At this point, you can wrap them well with plastic wrap and foil and refrigerate for up to 5 days. To serve, prepare the praline topping, spoon it over the cold cheesecakes, and return to the refrigerator so the topping can cool and harden, about 10 minutes. Remove from the refrigerator about 5 minutes before serving.

MAMA'S CHOCOLATE PIE *with* MERINGUE TOPPING

SERVES 6

1 cup sugar

¼ cup all-purpose flour

3 tablespoons unsweetened cocoa powder

¼ teaspoon kosher salt

2 cups whole milk

4 large egg yolks

2 tablespoons salted butter

½ teaspoon vanilla extract

1 Perfect Piecrust, prebaked and cooled (page 100)

Mile-High Meringue (page 192)

One bite of this silky pie and I'm in chocolate heaven! Although the chocolate is rich, the meringue is light as air. Whenever Mama made her chocolate pie as I was growing up, I couldn't wait until time to dig into a slice. I've updated her recipe by reducing the amount of butter. If you are a chocolate lover, this one's for you!

1 Preheat the oven to 375°F.

2 In a large saucepan set over medium heat, combine the sugar, flour, cocoa, and salt and stir well. Add 1 cup of the milk and stir until all the dry ingredients are mixed well. Add the remaining milk and mix thoroughly. Cook, stirring constantly, until the mixture begins to boil and becomes very thick, about 10 minutes.

3 In a small bowl, whisk the egg yolks. Pour about ½ cup of the hot chocolate mixture into the egg yolks, whisking constantly. Pour all of the egg mixture back into the milk mixture and cook, whisking constantly, until it begins to boil, about 2 minutes. Remove the pan from the heat and stir in the butter and vanilla. Pour into the prepared piecrust. Cover the pie filling with the meringue, making sure to spread it all the way to the edges of the crust.

4 Bake until the meringue is golden brown, 8 to 10 minutes. Transfer the pie to a wire rack and let cool to room temperature. Then refrigerate until cool, for at least 1 hour, before serving.

freezer friendly

For freezing, pour the cooked filling into the baked pie crust and allow to cool completely. Do not add the meringue. Wrap tightly with aluminum foil or plastic wrap, making sure to wrap all the way around the top and bottom of the pie. Store in a freezer bag in the freezer for up to 3 months. Thaw overnight in the refrigerator. Preheat the oven to 375°F. Prepare the meringue and spread on top of the pie filling, making sure to spread all the way to the edges of the crust. Bake until the meringue is golden brown, about 8 minutes.

MIMI'S PECAN PIE

SERVES 8

½ cup granulated sugar

3 large eggs

1 cup maple syrup

8 tablespoons (1 stick)
salted butter, melted

1 teaspoon vanilla extract

Pinch of kosher salt

1¼ cups pecan halves
or pieces

1 unbaked Perfect Piecrust
(page 100)

Like all of her grandchildren and great grandchildren, I knew my husband's grandmother as Mimi. I associate a few key things with Mimi: strands of fresh popcorn garland around a Christmas tree, white hair and the clearest blue eyes, Airstreams, and pecan pie. While her version uses the traditional light corn syrup (and you're welcome to substitute), I use maple syrup to stick with natural ingredients.

1 Preheat the oven to 350°F.

2 In a large bowl, whisk together the granulated sugar and eggs. Whisk in the maple syrup, melted butter, vanilla, and salt. Stir in the pecans and pour into the piecrust.

3 Bake until the center of the pie is set, 45 minutes to 1 hour. If the edges are browning too quickly, put a piece of foil over the top of the pie for the last few minutes of baking. Let cool completely before cutting and serving.

freezer friendly

Let the baked pie cool completely. Wrap tightly with aluminum foil or plastic wrap, making sure to wrap all the way around the top and bottom of the pie. Store in a freezer bag in the freezer for up to 3 months. Thaw overnight in the refrigerator, cut, and serve!

southern hospitality

To serve practically perfect slices of pecan pie every time, use a serrated knife and cut two slices of pie before serving one!

COCONUT CUSTARD PIE

SERVES 8

1 cup granulated sugar

1½ cups sweetened flaked coconut

¼ cup buttermilk

3 large eggs

6 tablespoons salted butter, melted

1 teaspoon vanilla extract

1 unbaked Perfect Piecrust (page 100)

This is the family pie recipe that I turn to time and again when I need something easy to whip together, and it's nice for all sorts of occasions. While the original recipe was delicious, it was always a bit too sweet for my taste. So I reduced the amount of the sugar, sweetened coconut, and butter. Now I love this pie even more!

1   Preheat the oven to 325°F.

2   In a large bowl, combine the sugar, coconut, buttermilk, eggs, butter, and vanilla. Pour into the piecrust.

3   Bake until the top is golden brown and the center is set, about 45 minutes. Let cool completely before serving.

freezer friendly
Let the baked pie cool completely. Wrap tightly with aluminum foil or plastic wrap, making sure to wrap all the way around the top and bottom of the pie. Store in a freezer bag in the freezer for up to 3 months. Thaw overnight in the refrigerator, cut, and serve!

GEORGIA PEACH CRISP

SERVES 6 TO 8

5 tablespoons salted butter, at room temperature

4 cups peeled and sliced fresh peaches (about 6 peaches)

¾ cup packed dark brown sugar

½ cup all-purpose flour

1 cup chopped pecans

½ teaspoon kosher salt

Vanilla ice cream, for serving (optional)

If there is one fruit that you can count on my family devouring, it's peaches. I practically stalk our local farmer's market, waiting for them to arrive each summer. Sweet and juicy, they're absolutely divine in all sorts of dishes, from appetizers to desserts. But let me tell you, if you are looking for a dessert that will garner umms, ahhhs, and more yums than you can imagine, this peach crisp is your ticket! I use less butter and sugar than traditional recipes, leaving you with the heady taste of peaches instead of sugar. If peaches are not in season, you can substitute another in-season fruit such as apples, pears, blueberries, or blackberries. For apple and pear crisps, I like to add ½ teaspoon of ground cinnamon.

1   Preheat the oven to 350°F. Line a rimmed baking sheet with foil (to catch anything that might bubble over).

2   In a 12-inch ovenproof skillet set over medium heat, melt 1 tablespoon of the butter. Add the peaches and ¼ cup of the brown sugar. Cook, stirring, until the juices thicken into a light syrup, about 8 minutes. Remove the pan from the heat.

3   In a medium bowl, combine the remaining 4 tablespoons butter, the remaining ½ cup brown sugar, the flour, pecans, and salt. Spread the mixture over the peaches. Place the skillet on the lined baking sheet.

4   Bake until golden brown and bubbly, about 30 minutes. Serve warm.

freezer friendly

Let the cooked peach crisp cool completely. Wrap tightly in plastic wrap, then foil. Store in a freezer bag in the freezer for up to 3 months. To serve, thaw in the refrigerator overnight. Reheat in a 350°F oven until warmed through, 10 to 15 minutes.

MAMA'S CREAM CHEESE POUND CAKE

SERVES 12

Baking spray

3 sticks salted butter, at room temperature

1 (8-ounce) package of cream cheese, at room temperature

3 cups granulated sugar

6 large eggs, at room temperature

3 cups all-purpose flour

1 teaspoon kosher salt

1 tablespoon vanilla extract

Mama went back to school and earned her nursing degree when I was just a little girl. She worked in hospitals and health care administration until well after I was grown. The hospital dietician gave her this recipe, which Mama has made frequently ever since. It's also the first cake she taught me to make as a little girl. I've since updated the recipe, replacing the margarine with butter for a more natural fat. It is simply scrumptious and easy as can be!

1   Preheat the oven to 325°F. Spray a 12-cup Bundt or tube pan well with baking spray or grease with softened butter and dust with flour, making sure to coat well to prevent any sticking.

2   In a stand mixer fitted with the paddle attachment (or using a hand mixer), beat the butter, cream cheese, and sugar until fluffy, about 3 minutes. Add the eggs one at a time, beating after each addition until well combined. Add the flour, salt, and vanilla and beat until well blended but do not overmix. Pour into the prepared pan.

3   Bake until the top is golden brown, the cake springs back when lightly pressed, and a wooden toothpick inserted into the center comes out clean, 1½ hours. Let cool for 10 minutes on a wire rack, and then turn the cake out onto the rack to cool completely.

freezer friendly
Let the cake cool completely. Wrap tightly with plastic wrap, then foil. Store in a freezer bag and freeze for up to 3 months. To serve, unwrap and allow to thaw completely before slicing.

SOUTHERN PANTRY

SO SIMPLE FREEZER JAM

**MAKES SEVEN
8-OUNCE JARS;
ABOUT 6½ CUPS**

4 cups pureed fruit
(strawberries, peaches,
blueberries, and
blackberries all work well)

1 tablespoon fresh
lemon juice

¾ cup unsweetened
apple juice

1 cup sugar

1 (1.75-ounce) package
of no-sugar-needed
powdered pectin

Although this recipe is called freezer jam, I admit that a few jars never even see my freezer. I always like to put one or two right in the refrigerator to use with biscuits (page 174), on toast, and in sandwiches. Pureeing fruit at its peak is the secret to using less sugar in this jam.

1 In a small bowl, combine the pureed fruit and the lemon juice.

2 In a 3-quart saucepan set over medium heat, bring the apple juice to a boil. Boil for 1 minute. Stir in the fruit puree and bring the mixture back to a boil. Stir in the sugar and again bring the mixture to a boil. Stir in the pectin and boil for 1 minute.

3 Remove the pan from the heat and ladle the mixture into sterilized jelly jars, leaving ½ inch of space at the top of each jar. Put the lids on the jars and tighten until just finger tight. Set in a cool space and do not move them until the jars have sealed, about 24 hours (see "How to Test Whether Jars Are Sealed Properly" on page 218).

4 Put the jars in the freezer; they'll keep for up to 1 year. To use, thaw in the refrigerator overnight and use within 3 weeks of opening.

sterilize jars and lids

It is very important to sterilize the jars and lids you plan to use for canning. There are various methods, and I recommend following the USDA canning guidelines for optimum food safety (http://nchfp.uga.edu/). With that in mind, here's how I prepare my jars and lids for canning.

- Gather all of your materials before you begin. You will need canning jars, flat canning lids, rings, a jar funnel, jar lifter, lid lifter, large stockpot or water bath canner, saucepan, rimmed baking sheet, clean dish towel(s), hot pads, and a little patience!

- Wash the canning jars, flat canning lids, and rings in hot, soapy water. Rinse well and dry the rings.

- With the mouth of the jars facing up, place the jars in a large stockpot or water bath canner. Fill the stockpot with warm water to cover the tops of the jars by at least 1 inch. Bring the water to a boil and boil for 10 minutes, timing carefully. (Check the USDA guidelines for modifications needed if you are at an elevation higher than 1,000 feet.) Reduce the heat to a simmer and leave the jars in the simmering water, removing them one at a time as you are ready to fill each jar.

- Meanwhile, put the flat lids in a small saucepan set over medium heat and bring to a simmer, no more than 180 degrees. Be careful not to let the water boil as it will damage the seal! Leave the flat lids in the simmering water, removing one at a time as you are ready to place it on a filled jar.

- Using the jar lifter, remove one hot jar from the stockpot. Pour the water in the jar back into the stockpot.

- Using a jar funnel, fill the jar with your contents, leaving the amount of headspace at the top according to the recipe you are using.

- Using the lid lifter, remove a hot flat lid (again, remove only one at a time) from the hot water in the saucepan. Place the lid on top of the jar and carefully screw on the ring. Adjust until it is finger tight. Do not overtighten.

- Using a hot pad or the jar lifter, carefully place the filled jar on the towel-lined baking sheet.

- Repeat until all jars are filled, making sure that the jars do not touch. Unless you are processing the jars in a water bath, do not move the jars for at least 24 hours and check that each jar has sealed before storing (see the sealing test under "How to Can Foods in a Water Bath," page 218).

SWEET *and* SPICY BBQ SAUCE

MAKES 1 CUP

1 cup tomato sauce, homemade (page 229) or store-bought

3 tablespoons apple cider vinegar

¼ cup molasses

2 tablespoons honey or packed dark brown sugar

2 tablespoons Worcestershire sauce

½ teaspoon onion powder

½ teaspoon garlic powder

½ teaspoon kosher salt

¼ teaspoon freshly ground black pepper

⅛ teaspoon cayenne pepper

I love to stir this barbecue sauce into shredded Perfect Pork Roast (page 81) for making pulled pork sandwiches or slather it onto Mama's Meat Loaf (page 109). The blend of sweet and spicy is delicious! While this barbecue sauce is fast and freezer friendly, it's also fantastic for canning. Just cook the sauce according to the recipe instructions and process following the water bath canning method (page 218), leaving ½ inch of headspace and processing for 20 minutes in the water bath. It makes a great gift!

1   In a small saucepan set over medium heat, combine the tomato sauce, vinegar, molasses, honey, Worcestershire sauce, onion powder, garlic powder, salt, black pepper, and cayenne. Bring to a low boil and cook until thickened, about 10 minutes. Reduce the heat to low and simmer until the sauce coats the back of a spoon, about 5 more minutes.

2   If not using right away, let cool completely before transferring to a glass jar and storing in the refrigerator for up to 2 weeks.

freezer friendly
Let the sauce cool completely. Pour it into an airtight, freezer-safe container. Freeze for up to 3 months. To use, let thaw in the refrigerator overnight.

GRAND-MOTHER'S DILL PICKLES

Every summer, my sister, Wendy, and I would watch Grandmother Verdie make these dill pickles again and again and again until a whole shelf in her pantry was filled. We knew that, no matter how many she put away, we'd have that shelf depleted well before pickling time the next summer! They're simple to make and classic.

MAKES 4 PINT JARS

2½ pounds (3- to 5-inch) pickling cucumbers

2 bunches of fresh dill

½ teaspoon Ball Pickle Crisp (optional)

2¼ cups distilled white vinegar

2 tablespoons pickling salt

1   Scrub the cucumbers with a soft brush under running water until clean. Trim both ends off each cucumber and quarter each cucumber lengthwise making spears. Pack the cucumbers into hot, sterilized jars (follow the instructions on page 216). Place 2 sprigs of fresh dill into each jar and add ⅛ teaspoon of pickle crisp per jar if using.

2   In a large nonreactive saucepan set over medium heat, combine 2½ cups water with the vinegar and pickling salt. Bring to a boil. Pour the boiling liquid over the cucumbers and dill, leaving ½ inch of headspace at the top of the jar. Use the water bath canning process for 10 minutes.

3   Check that the jars have sealed properly (see below) before storing in a cool, dry place. Unopened, they'll keep for at least 1 year. Refrigerate opened jars for up to 6 months.

HOW TO
can foods in a water bath

If the recipe requires water bath canning, use the jar lifter to transfer the filled and sealed jars back into the stockpot of simmering water. Once all the jars are in the stockpot, bring the heat up to a boil and boil according to your recipe instructions. Make sure that the jars remain upright at all times and be careful when you add and remove the jars from the boiling water.

Once the jars have boiled for the length of time specified in your recipe, turn off the heat and let the water cool for 5 to 10 minutes. Line the baking sheet with the towel. Then, using the jar lifter, remove each jar and place it on the towel, leaving about an inch between jars. Do not move the jars for at least 24 hours and check that each jar has sealed before storing.

HOW TO TEST WHETHER JARS ARE SEALED PROPERLY
There are two ways that I test jars for proper sealing. First, gently press the middle of the flat canning lid with your finger—it should not spring back. Second, the flat canning lid should have an indentation in the center if sealed properly.

PEPPER JELLY

MAKES FOUR
½-PINT JARS
(ABOUT 4 CUPS)

1½ cups seeded and
chopped sweet bell peppers
(red, orange, and/or yellow,
2 to 3 medium peppers)

½ cup seeded and chopped
green bell pepper
(about 1 medium pepper)

1 jalapeño pepper, seeded
and finely chopped

½ cup apple cider vinegar

2½ cups sugar

1 (1.75-ounce) package of
low-sugar or no-sugar-
needed powdered pectin

Whatever else you do, will you please make this pepper jelly? Just once. And when you do, will you also please make all of the recipes in this cookbook that call for it, from the Pepper Jelly Pork Medallions (page 56) to the Pepper Jelly Vinaigrette (page 166)? Oh, and don't forget to add a spoonful to your peas, beans, or greens (delicious!). But make sure to keep a jar or two in the pantry to use for a last-minute appetizer on top of cream cheese. I have a feeling that you'll love it as much as I do!

1   In a large stockpot set over medium heat, combine all of the peppers and the vinegar. Bring the mixture to a rolling boil that does not stop bubbling when stirred. Boil for 1 minute, stirring constantly. Add the sugar and stir until dissolved. Cook until the mixture returns to a rolling boil. Boil for 1 minute, stirring constantly. Stir in the pectin and bring back up to a rolling boil. Boil for 1 minute. Remove the pan from the heat.

2   Pour the jelly into sterilized jars (see page 216), leaving ½ inch headspace at the top of each jar. Follow the water bath canning instructions (page 218) and process for 10 minutes.

3   Store in the pantry, unopened, for up to 1 year. Once opened, store in the refrigerator for up to 3 weeks.

SWEET TEA CONCENTRATE

MAKES 4 CUPS CONCENTRATE; 16 SERVINGS

4 family-size tea bags

1 to 1½ cups sugar

Pinch of baking soda

On family reunion day, Grandmother would spread towels in the back of her car and then pack it basket by basket, dish by dish, and plate by plate until filled to the brim. But, as delicious as everything was, I always dreaded riding with her and Granddaddy to the reunion. You see, my sister and I were responsible for making sure that the many gallons of tea she'd made didn't tip and spill on the ride! Fast-forward a few decades, when our friend Christy taught me about sweet tea concentrate. One recipe makes sixteen individual servings or a gallon of tea, and it is so much easier to keep in the refrigerator—or take along with you to family reunions! For me it was a revelation. The baking soda makes the tea less bitter and keeps it from becoming cloudy.

1. Bring 1 quart water to a boil in a medium saucepan set over medium heat. Remove the pan from the heat and drop in the tea bags. Let steep for 15 minutes.

2. Meanwhile, put the sugar (more or less, depending on how sweet you want it) in a 1-quart Mason jar. Remove the tea bags, carefully pressing the bags against the side of the saucepan before discarding them. Pour a little of the tea into the Mason jar and stir until the sugar has dissolved. Pour in the remaining tea. Stir in the baking soda, which prevents the tea from becoming cloudy and bitter, and screw the lid on the jar tightly. The concentrate will keep in the refrigerator for up to 2 weeks.

3. To make a glass of tea from this concentrate, pour ¼ cup of the concentrate into a glass, add ice, and fill with ¾ cup cold water. To make a gallon, pour all of the concentrate into a gallon pitcher and fill with cold water.

APPLE BUTTER

MAKES 2 ½ CUPS

3 pounds (6 large or 9 medium) Macintosh or Honeycrisp apples, peeled, cored, and chopped

¾ cup packed dark brown sugar

¾ cup granulated sugar

1 teaspoon ground cinnamon

¼ teaspoon ground allspice

⅛ teaspoon grated nutmeg

⅛ teaspoon ground ginger

⅛ teaspoon kosher salt

The traditional way of making apple butter is to let the apples and spices cook on the stove for hours—and boy, does the bubbling mixture sure splatter all over the stove! To cut down on the time spent watching over it, as well as to eliminate the mess, I came up with this version. I love that I can toss all of the ingredients into the slow cooker in the evening and wake up the next morning to apple butter ready for pureeing! It's delicious in the Cinnamon Apple Shortcakes (page 200) or simply stirred into a bowl of steel-cut oats.

1   Put the apples, brown sugar, granulated sugar, cinnamon, allspice, nutmeg, ginger, and salt in a slow cooker. Stir well.

2   Cover and cook on low for 10 hours. Using an immersion blender, carefully blend the mixture until the apple butter is smooth. Alternatively, carefully transfer the fruit in batches to a food processor or blender and puree.

3   Pour the apple butter into pint jars, leaving about ½ inch of space at the top of the jar. The apple butter will keep in the refrigerator for up to 2 weeks.

freezer friendly
Store jars of apple butter in the freezer for up to 3 months. To use, thaw overnight in the refrigerator.

ESSENTIAL SEASONINGS *and* SPICE BLENDS

I love to use herbs, seasonings, and spices in my cooking; these are a few favorites that I make and keep on hand for quick, flavorful weeknight meals.

STONE HOUSE SEASONING

MAKES ABOUT ½ CUP

¼ cup kosher salt

2 tablespoons freshly ground black pepper

2 teaspoons granulated garlic or 1 teaspoon garlic powder

In a small bowl, combine the salt, pepper, and granulated garlic. The blend will keep in an airtight container for at least 1 year. Use with beef, poultry, pork, and vegetables.

BLACKENING SEASONING

MAKES ABOUT ½ CUP

2 tablespoons paprika

2 teaspoons kosher salt

2 teaspoons freshly ground black pepper

2 teaspoons cayenne pepper

2 teaspoons ground cumin

2 teaspoons dried thyme

1 teaspoon onion powder

1 teaspoon garlic powder

1 teaspoon dried oregano

In a small bowl, combine the paprika, salt, black pepper, cayenne pepper, cumin, thyme, onion powder, garlic powder, and oregano. The blend will keep in an airtight container for at least 1 year. Use with fish, chicken, and vegetables.

ESPRESSO CHILI SPICE BLEND

MAKES ABOUT ½ CUP

¼ cup chili powder

2 tablespoons espresso powder or instant espresso

2 tablespoons packed dark brown sugar

1½ teaspoons kosher salt

1 teaspoon freshly ground black pepper

1 teaspoon paprika

1 teaspoon ground cumin

In a small bowl, combine the chili powder, espresso powder, sugar, salt, pepper, paprika, and cumin. The blend will keep in an airtight container for up to 1 year. Use with steaks, roasts, and chilis.

DRY RUB MIX

MAKES ABOUT ½ CUP

2 tablespoons packed dark brown sugar

2 tablespoons kosher salt

1 tablespoon freshly ground black pepper

1 tablespoon paprika

1 teaspoon granulated garlic or 1 teaspoon garlic powder

¼ to ½ teaspoon cayenne pepper

In a small bowl, combine the sugar, salt, black pepper, paprika, garlic, and cayenne pepper (use the higher amount if you want it spicier). The blend will keep well in an airtight container for up to 1 year. Use with beef, pork, chicken, and fish.

southern hospitality

These rubs and spice blends make wonderful housewarming, hostess, and holiday gifts. Simply portion into small, clean spice jars and affix a label with the name of the spice.

HOW TO
blanch tomatoes for easy peeling

Fill a large saucepan three-quarters full with water and
bring to rolling boil. Fill a second large pan with ice
water. Score a small *x* on the bottom of each tomato.
Place the tomatoes in the boiling water for 30 seconds.
Using a slotted spoon, immediately transfer the
tomatoes to the ice water and submerge them for 30
seconds. They'll be very easy to peel now!

HOMEMADE FRESH TOMATO SAUCE

MAKES 2 PINTS

4 pounds tomatoes, peeled
(see sidebar), seeded,
and chopped

2 teaspoons fresh
lemon juice

½ teaspoon kosher salt

There is nothing like tomato sauce made with the very freshest tomatoes. A staple for so many recipes, this sauce is stockpiled in my freezer. When tomatoes are at their peak, I set aside some time to put up a bunch of sauce so that I can capture the very best flavor. You can use whichever tomatoes you have on hand or prefer, but plum tomatoes are my favorite. I don't put any seasonings in my recipe so that I can use the sauce in a wider variety of ways—from Easy Skillet Lasagna (page 74) to Brisket with Tomato Gravy (page 84).

1   In a large, heavy-bottomed stockpot or Dutch oven set over medium-low heat, bring the tomatoes to a simmer and cook until thickened, 30 minutes. Remove the pan from the heat and stir in the lemon juice and salt. Using a potato masher, immersion blender, or food processor, process until the sauce has a smooth consistency. Let cool completely.

2   The sauce will keep in airtight containers in the refrigerator for up to 1 week.

freezer friendly

Pour the cooled tomato sauce into freezer-safe bags or containers. Freeze for up to 3 months. To use, simply thaw in the refrigerator overnight.

For smaller servings, ladle the sauce into ice cube trays and flash freeze for 30 minutes. Transfer the cubes to sealable freezer bags and freeze for up to 3 months. To use, toss a cube of tomato sauce into recipes as needed. Each cube should equal about 2 tablespoons of tomato sauce.

CHOW CHOW

MAKES 8
HALF-PINT JARS

2 medium green bell
peppers, seeded and
finely chopped

1 medium red bell pepper,
seeded and finely chopped

2 small hot peppers, seeded
and finely chopped

2 small green tomatoes,
finely chopped

2 cups finely chopped plum
tomatoes (about 6)

2 cups finely chopped
onions (about 2 medium)

2 cups finely chopped
green cabbage

1 cup sugar

1 cup distilled white vinegar

2 teaspoons kosher salt

If you've never eaten chow chow, then this is the time to give it a try! Chow chow is a classic Southern condiment used to top peas, beans, or greens (try it on Field Peas and Snaps, page 148), but one of my favorite ways to eat it is alongside Perfect Pork Roast (page 81). Mercy!

1   In a large stockpot set over medium heat, combine all the peppers, the green and plum tomatoes, the onions, cabbage, sugar, vinegar, and salt. Bring the mixture to a boil. Reduce the heat to low, cover, and simmer for 30 minutes. Uncover the pot and simmer for an additional 30 minutes, or until thick.

2   Pour the chow chow into sterilized jars (see page 216), leaving ½ inch headspace at the top of each jar. Follow the water bath canning instructions (page 218) and process for 10 minutes. Place in a cool spot and let sit for 24 hours. Store in the pantry, unopened, for up to 1 year. Once opened, store in the refrigerator for up to 3 months.

ACKNOWLEDGMENTS

This cookbook was written with a whole lot of love, laughter, and yes, even a few tears along the way as I sifted through recipe notes of Grandmother Verdie's. One thing is for certain—it would not have been possible without a lot of love, encouragement, and help!

TO ALL THE *ADD A PINCH* **FAMILY:** Your loyalty, support, and love mean the world and made this book possible. I hope that you love this book as much as I've loved writing it for you and that your book is splattered, stained, and well worn from use!

TO BART AND SAM: Thank you for loving me, for being the best family any girl could hope for, and for being my favorite taste testers. You two are the best! I love you!

TO MAMA: Thank you for everything. I don't know what I would do without you! You are truly an angel among us. I still hope that I grow up to be like you.

TO DADDY: Thank you for always making me believe that anything is possible with faith and hard work; for telling me to do the right thing, even if no one is watching; to be sweet, even when faced with sour; to be strong, even when I don't feel like it; and to love like there is no tomorrow. I'll always be Daddy's girl.

TO WENDY, MY SISTER AND BEST FRIEND: How in the world I was blessed with such an amazing sister, I'll never know! I just thank my lucky stars that I was. Love you!

TO MY MOTHER-IN-LAW AND FATHER-IN-LAW, TISH AND BOB: Thank you for raising such a wonderful man. I pray I do as well with my son as you have done with Bart.

TO MY BEST BUDDY, AMY, who surely feels more like a sister than a friend ever should: You are the best!

TO MARIA, ASHLEY, STEPHANIE, HELENE, CARRIE, GINNY, AND ANNA KATE: Thank you for making this book come to life. Your vision, infectious enthusiasm, and incredible talent are unparalleled! I'm so honored to have worked with each of you, but I'm even more honored to now call you friends.

Thank you to my family and friends for always being such cheerleaders and supporters. You mean so much to me! Steve, Katherine, the Stones, Robin, Penny, the Dukes, the McMichaels, the Whitworths, Nola, Ree, Gina, Jaden, Christy, Bridget, Rebecca, Sandy, Wendy, Angie, Lori, Kate, Amanda, Kristen, and the whole blogging community.

ICON INDEX

INDEX

Crackers - Toss in
Spread on cookie she...
dry in low oven
or food storage

chill - Pour in pan...
bowl over ice - add
large bottle ginger...
Stir well.
Makes 1 1/2 gal.

2 sticks of margarine
1 C. crunchy peanut butter
Pour in bowl with
2 cups graham cracker crumbs
and 3 cups of confectionate sug
press in 9 x 11 pan.
Melt 6 oz. semi sweet choc.
and 2 Tabs. of shortening
in microwave 2 min. and
and smooth over topp and
Chill.

Reece's

Strawberry pie
1 Baked
Box (Crunchy)